My Life Extraordinary

at

The BBC

Grant Bremner

Copyright © 2023 Grant Bremner

All rights reserved. No part of this publication may be reproduced, stored in a retrieval system, or transmitted in any form or by any means, electronic, mechanical, photocopying, recording, or otherwise, without the prior permission of the author.

ISBN: 9798857261576

Disclaimer

This account of my working life at the BBC and being a trade union representative within the organisation is completely written from memory at least forty years after the events described and in some cases add another twenty years. Therefore, there may be some inaccuracies in dates and events for which I sincerely apologise, and there are some surnames that I have simply forgotten due to a failing memory at my age. I have tried my best to write an accurate version of my life as it happened while working for the BBC over a period of 30 extraordinary years.

Grant Bremner
2023

ABOUT THE AUTHOR

Grant Bremner was born in Aberdeen, Scotland, but spent his entire working life with the BBC, mostly in London, in a variety of positions with film and television.

He took early retirement due to a worsening back condition and he and his wife Sue moved to Spain where he began to write seriously. They returned to the UK 20 years later in time for the publication of his first paperback, The Quest for the Holey Pail, in 2013. Since then he has continued writing and has published an extensive range of novels and short stories in several genres. More of his work can be found at Amazon.co.uk.

For more information visit his website:

www.grantbremner.co.uk

DEDICATION

To my wife Sue for her invaluable help and unstinting support during my writing years and longer. Without such support I would not have had the inclination or the inspiration to put together this story of my working life at the BBC. My sincere and heartfelt thanks.

How it Started

My career with the BBC began due to a couple of rather peculiar and what I would call extremely unpredictable circumstances. I had left Kaimhill Senior Secondary school at the age of fifteen in 1959 and I enrolled in the Aberdeen Wireless College located in Albyn Terrace, my clear intention being to become a wireless operator in the merchant navy. As a Scot I obviously had the wanderlust as I wanted to travel the world using my position aboard a merchant vessel. There were eight other aspiring radio operators in my class and we set about learning the basics of Morse code immediately on our very first day. We would practise to begin with on dummy keypads with a pair of rather uncomfortable and heavy headphones listening to ourselves for two hours in the morning and again for the same period of time in the afternoon.

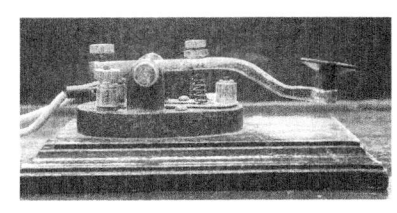

We were all relieved when lectures broke the tedious monotonous routine of practising Morse code by oneself. Mr Martin, who I and the other students had hoped would regale us with his adventures on the high seas, informed us that prior to becoming a teacher in wireless technology he had spent his career at the Coast Guard Station and had never been to sea, although he had travelled on the ferry from Glasgow to Rothesay on several occasions. With our mouths ajar at this very disappointing revelation he started on our first lecture regarding the transmission of radio waves.

I must admit that my notebook contained very few notes on that particular lecture as I assume my brain was busy processing the shocking revelation that we were going to be taught by a man who had never been to sea.

As the months passed we all progressed to transmitting stories from the local morning newspaper via our Morse keypads to another student picked by Mr Martin to listen to our output and write down the results. To be honest I much preferred to do the transmission rather than the listening as I considered myself to be pretty fast on the keypad, and on occasion would see a look of fear and confusion on the face of the student opposite me as he tried his utmost to keep track of my Morse as my thumb and first finger fairly raced on.

Wireless technology back in the late fifties was, needless to say, not as sophisticated as we have today. Radios were of course valves, resistors with simple circuit boards that we would practice taking to pieces and putting back together under the watchful eye of our teacher. With winter approaching we were all informed in the first week of December that we were required to have an eye test. So off I went to a specialist eye-testing centre armed with the appropriate form from the college which needed to be completed. I was surprised when the final part of the test was in a darkened room where coloured pinpricks of light were displayed on a screen and you had to identify the two different colours.

I was further shocked to be informed by the examiner that I had failed the test due to what he called 'a degree of colour blindness.' He went on to say that perhaps my eyes were tired and that I should rest them for a week by not doing any more transmissions of the newspapers and to return in a week for another test. At that stage I was not too concerned as he gave the clear impression all would be well. However, one week later I emerged holding the form with Colour Blindness stamped on it, I had failed the test again.

The following morning I handed the form to the Principal of the Aberdeen Wireless College who looked at it then explained that as I had failed the test and could not determine between white and red at the required distance of three miles I would never be able to have a career in the merchant navy. Beaming a broad smile he then said, 'Never mind Grant, you can still join the Coast Guard,' and my world fell apart there and then.

On my way home on the bus I resolved to inform my parents that I would be leaving the college as I did not want to have a job in the Coast Guard. They took the news quite well although my mum did her best during the evening to dissuade me from leaving the college and said I should think it over during the weekend. Over the next couple of days my resolve hardened, and I was most annoyed that the Wireless College had not thought it prudent to have the students eye tested at the very beginning of term. So it was that first thing on Monday morning at 9am I entered the principal's office and told him I was leaving immediately.

He was not best pleased, told me I was being stupid and that he would require confirmation from my parents. I collected my meagre belongings, my headphones, a lighter pair purchased by me, plus a few notebooks and left the building. I was home when he eventually contacted my father who confirmed my decision was supported and he went on to tell him that the eye tests, being so vitally important for the merchant navy, should in his opinion have been conducted prior to the commencement of term. I have to say I was proud of my dad, although mum was still concerned about my future prospects, work was hard to come by in Aberdeen for any youngster back then.

Later that evening after dinner my dad, who was reading the Evening Express, an evening newspaper, turned to me and said, 'There's a job at the BBC, that's radio, the same sort of thing you've been studying.' The job in fact was for an Office Junior at the BBC 36 Beechgrove Terrace which in 1959 was only a radio station. I had left college and had no job prospects so I got pen and paper and proceeded to write an application letter which I posted the following day, hardly expecting to get an interview. However, the following Monday I received a typed letter inviting me to an interview that Friday morning at 10.30am. I arrived a few minutes early and sat nervously wondering what I would say if I was asked why I had spurned a career in the Coast Guard.

A lady by the name of Stella Campbell introduced herself and escorted me into the large office of Harry Hoggan the BBC's Aberdeen Representative.

I noticed he had my letter on his desk which he barely glanced at. 'Grant I have one question to ask, can you fill in a football coupon?' he said looking directly at me. 'Of course sir, I do it for my dad every Friday,' I replied instantly, although I had never actually filled in a football coupon. My dad did his own coupons.

4

'Thank you, we'll let you know.' The interview was concluded after less than a couple of minutes. On the bus on my way home I reasoned that I had better start looking in the local papers to see if there was any work going for a young boy six months out of school. My parents found it difficult to comprehend that I had only been asked that one question about the coupon but I insisted it was the truth.

A few days later a letter stamped with the BBC crest arrived addressed to me and with trepidation I opened it expecting to see a rejection letter but my eyes opened wide when I read that I had been appointed and that I should attend for duty on Monday 18th January and that I should be attired in a suit. My starting salary would be 3 pounds and 14 shillings per week. I noticed 'cont..' at the foot of the page so I turned it over and was surprised to read that my appointment was only until my 18th birthday. There had been no mention of this in the advert in the newspaper or at my brief interview. Still I had a job for the next two and a half years. It never entered my head that the BBC would be my only employer until I retired on health grounds nearly 30 years later.

Of course being away from the Wireless College I was the only person at home when my letter arrived and when my mother returned from her home care job, the instant she opened the front door I handed her the letter from the BBC even though she still had a carrier bag with shopping in her other hand. 'I got the job at the BBC mum, I start next Monday,' I said quickly with excitement before she even had time to read the letter. She dropped the shopping bag and gave me a big hug then said, 'I expect your father will be pleased, well done Grant.'

When father arrived home from his Tailoring job mum was in the kitchen where the family ate all our meals preparing dinner. I waited until he had sat down in his favourite armchair adjacent to the burning coal fire, remember it was 15th January in 1960, there was snow on the ground and it was bitterly cold outside. I handed him the letter which he read slowly, looked into the fire then said, 'As you start with the BBC on Monday, I'm sorry but I can't make you a new suit in two days. So tomorrow morning we'll take the bus into town and see what Burtons have in their winter sale.'

During dinner it was my dad who announced to my elder brother Bruce and his twin sister Rosemary that I was starting work at the BBC next week. My sister said 'well done Grant,' but Bruce only scowled at me then left the table giving me a hard slap across my shoulder that stung, clearly he was not pleased for me. Nevertheless, it did not dampen my spirits and so it was that dad and I set off by bus the following morning to visit the Burtons men's clothes shop in George Street.

There was indeed a winter sale with certain suits marked down by either 10 or 15 percent. I was quite impressed by a bright blue suit and wanted to try it on but my dad said no as it was far too colourful for an office job. I must admit that I was rather disappointed but gave in to his experience and expertise as a tailor and after half an hour or so we left the shop with a paper bag containing a dark blue suit that cost 14 pounds and 6 shillings. The legs were slightly too long but my dad had turned down the offer from the salesman to have them altered, saying he would do them himself, which he did later that day using my mum's Singer pedal sewing machine. He even had the correct colour thread for the sewing.

So it was on Monday the 18th of January 1960 I left home and took two buses to get to the BBC 36 Beechgrove Terrace building, arriving early at 9.15am wanting to give a good impression.

The BBC building at 36 Beechgrove Terrace as it looked when I first arrived on 18th January 1960

I walked up what I considered a long driveway to the front door noting the elaborate pillars on each side and carried on through the impressive front door and approached the reception desk where two uniformed commissionaires stood behind a high desk, one tall the other quite short in stature.

'Ah, you'll be Grant, the new office junior, your initial workplace is behind the desk. My name is Gordon and this is Norman, we're going to show you the ropes, but first I'm going to take you on a tour of the building.'

The building was set within large grounds where the famous BBC Garden was produced several years later in the 70's which ran for many years, and it was an impressive large house with a plethora of offices spread over three floors plus a radio recording studio. We left the reception desk and turned right up a broad carpeted staircase that split about halfway up with a turning to the left leading to a few steps that led up to several offices. We went straight on up arriving at a corridor to the right where we passed by a small recording studio and then turned right again up some slighter steeper stairs arriving at what Gordon said was the most important room in the building, it was a small staff canteen where teas, coffees and even lunch could be purchased. I was very impressed indeed looking at the price list displayed, there would be no need to take sandwiches to work.

Gordon continued with the tour taking me back down the steep stairs and along another short corridor towards the rear of the building where there were another two offices plus a room with a full-sized billiard table. 'Can the staff use this Gordon,' I enquired eagerly.

'Yes', he replied. 'Can you play?' he asked.

'No,' I said with disappointment showing on my face.

'No worries young Grant. I'll be happy to teach you during your lunch break,' he replied.

Next we went to the small PABX office where I was informed by Janet that I would be required to operate the telephone system during her coffee breaks and lunch. She asked if it would be acceptable if she kept to the same time which was twelve to one. She went on to explain that she lived locally and always went home for lunch. I was happy to agree as I preferred the later time of one to two.

The switchboard looked complicated as I had never seen one before, but I quickly discovered that it was fairly easy to use by simply switching calls from outside the building by means of using plug in wires to the different extension required, similar to the one pictured.

Leaving the PABX room Gordon then took me to each office and introduced me to the secretaries, members of the radio production teams and finally into the Cashier's Office on the ground floor adjacent to the secretary to the Aberdeen Representative, Stella Campbell. Miss Johnson, the cashier, was a lady of small stature but I was soon to learn a hard yet very fair task master. Gordon left me in her office and went back to his duties on the front reception desk while Miss Johnson described what my duties regarding her office were to be.

1 I had to take cheques to the various companies the BBC had accounts with.

2 I had to collect various stationery supplies from a list of specific companies.

3 I had to collect money from Barclays Bank.

4 I was to collect any parcels from the Post Office.

5 I would be expected to go anywhere in Aberdeen to deliver specific letters.

6 I had to deliver the mail to the required offices.

'Today I have nothing for you, so you can return to the reception desk,' she concluded with a friendly smile.

The remainder of the day was spent mostly with familiarising myself with the building and receiving my first training session on the PABX system when I was told that it would be much better if I were to lose my fairly broad Aberdonian accent when answering incoming calls, after all I was an employee of the BBC. When I went home I explained to my family what my first day had been like and the duties that were expected of me. I did not mention the part about being instructed to lose my accent, that would not have gone down well, especially with my dad.

The months passed quickly, I soon knew the best and quickest way to take the cheques around Aberdeen using the various buses. Luckily there was a number 13 bus stop only a few yards from the end of the drive that took me down to Union Street, the main thoroughfare in Aberdeen. The newspaper office of The Press & Journal and the Evening Express was a frequent visit along with the Railway Station. I soon became acquainted with the staff in these offices, and of course the bus conductors who were still employed back then.

Gordon, the Commissionnaire, had kept his word and he insisted that we start with billiards as that would teach me how to get used to knowing where you wanted your white ball to be on the table when we started playing snooker. I have to admit that Gordon was a very good player indeed. He was also a member of the ABS (Association of Broadcasting Staff) the BBC Union. He asked me when I was about six months in the job if I would like to join. As he had been so kind to me during those first few months I said yes and duly signed the necessary form. Little did I know then how that decision, made at the age of sixteen, would affect my life in the BBC a few years later.

By the beginning of summer I had managed to lose my accent on the telephone yet managed to retain it at home. I was completely at ease putting plugs in and out and flicking switches without even looking. I also began learning to type in the small area behind the reception desk and this was to stand me in good stead later on.

A tiring machine at its best

I was amazed when I was informed by Stella at the beginning of May that I was entitled to two weeks holiday and that she would appreciate knowing when I'd like to take them. She went on to explain that I could of course take separate weeks if that suited me better. I decided to take two weeks off in June around my birthday and spend some time with my sister Edith who was living in Glasgow with her fireman husband Jock.

Possible Early End to my BBC Career:

One day in November around seven in the evening I was on my way from home to the fish and chip shop in Garthdee to buy a poke of chips when I was stopped by two plain clothes policemen and taken by car down to the small station at the Bridge of Dee. They did not tell me the reason why they wanted to talk to me until we arrived at the station. The conversation went along the following lines:
'What's your name boy?' asked the tall one as he bent right down to my ear.
'Grant Bremner,' I answered immediately.
'Grant Bremner is it?' enquired the shorter one who had his notebook out.
'Oh no it's William Grant Bremner,' I replied casually and truthfully.
'So you're a liar, are you,' yelled the other policeman at me.
'No, my dad's name is William so I get called Grant, always have been,' I replied, now feeling a bit nervous.
'Do you always give a different name when you get asked?' shouted the tall one into my ear.
'No of course not, it was a genuine mistake, sorry,' I responded.
'Right then William have you been smashing the lights on lampposts?' asked the short one as he sat down opposite me.
'No of course not.' I was amazed at the question.
'Do you know who has been then?' asked the tall one again loudly in my ear.
'No I didn't even know any had been broken,' I answered truthfully.
'Are you working?' shorty asked in a sneering kind of manner.

'I have a job at the BBC,' I replied truthfully.
'Another lie is it?' the taller one still standing right beside me asked. 'We will check you know.'
'I work at the BBC in Beechgrove Terrace,' I replied.
'Right then, you can go,' said the short one with the notebook.
I didn't need a second invitation and I was out the door as quick as I could. The whole incident lasted about twenty minutes from start to finish.

However, the following morning I was summoned to Harry Hoggan's office. 'Grant, the Chief Constable has informed me that you were interviewed by the police yesterday, please explain.'
I told him exactly what had happened and that I had absolutely nothing to do with broken lights in lampposts and that I was only on my way to buy some chips when I had been picked up. 'Well Grant, if the Chief Constable calls me again about you, you'll be out of here, understood?'
Even though I had done nothing wrong, from that day to this I have never fully trusted the police and for the next few months I was actually terrified I might be picked up again for no reason whatsoever. Had I been so, that would have been the end of my BBC career.

The rest of the year flew by and as January approached I realised that I had almost completed my first year working for the BBC. A snooker competition was held and of course Gordon won it handsomely but I was delighted that I was the runner up. A small Christmas office party was held which I thoroughly enjoyed as everyone was happy and cheerful. The BBC 36 Beechgrove Terrace was a wonderful and joyous place to work. I was very content and really happy with my work. Oops! I almost forgot, we had our very own BBC Club in a separate prefabricated building next to the rear gate.

In 1961 when I was seventeen I realised that I could now learn to drive a car. It so happened that the BBC had a Vanden Plas that was kept in a garage/workshop and only occasionally used by the handyman George. The car was only ever driven out and reversed back again, so I had an idea. Around September I asked Stella to find out, if I was able to pass my driving test, whether I would be allowed to use the car for my cheque deliveries into Aberdeen. The response was better than I expected from Harry Hoggan, Yes I could and they would also pay for my driving lessons. In January 1962 I managed to pass my driving test and thought I would be able to use the Vanden Plas but no, I had to wait until someone came up from the BBC in Glasgow to give me a test. It was April before he arrived, excited I got in the car and he sat beside me.

As I was approaching the open rear exit gate he said, 'Take a left.' So I drove into Beechgrove Gardens. 'Take another left,' he said, so I turned into Beechgrove Terrace. 'Take another left,' he said once more. I drove back up the drive of the BBC and parked the car by the garage. 'Good, you've passed, now where's the club?' I could not have travelled more than two hundred yards in total yet I had passed the BBC driving test.

The following week I began using the car every time I had to go into Aberdeen, it was such a change from getting on and off buses and parking was so much easier then.

Me on a day off visiting the BBC Club at Beechgrove Terrace.

Later in 1962 saw a major change ahead for the BBC in Aberdeen, we were informed that we were to become a television station in order to compete with the recently opened Grampian TV. It had been decided to build a small two-camera news studio on the site. We had only been a radio station since Beechgrove was opened in 1938. On 26 July 1962 the first live transmission, a two-minute insert into the Scottish News, was sent over the microwave link to Glasgow. Because there was a shortage of studio space in Glasgow at the time, it wasn't long before the studio in Aberdeen was doing a lot more than news, with programmes such as Religious Services and small LE shows which were quite a challenge to do since the technical facilities were very basic. Later, in 1964 (after I had transferred to London) the studio came into national prominence, when there was the serious outbreak of typhoid in Aberdeen, due, it was subsequently discovered, to a contaminated tin of corned beef! Suddenly it seemed like most of the world's reporters had descended on the studio to get their films processed and their reports transmitted. The discovery of oil and gas in the North Sea kept the newsroom and the studio busy for many years to come. I did however find it strange the first time I walked into the new television studio to see a grand piano sitting there. Little did I realise then that it would be used on a regular basis.

Anne and Laura Brand practising in the TV Studio in 1962

My duties did not change with the arrival of the television studio and life really went on as before, A dinner dance was held at Christmas and I invited a girl with whom I had won a 'rock 'n roll' competition at our community centre in Garthdee. Apparently the judge told Anne that it was her smile that had captivated him. Many years later we met again through Facebook and she told me she had thoroughly enjoyed the experience. We keep in touch today and she is a good friend.

As my 18th birthday approached I began to get nervous about leaving my post as office junior and began to look for another job. Then, out of the blue a personnel officer arrived from Glasgow and told me that, as I had such good annual reports, she was able to offer me a job in the post room in Glasgow. Instantly I knew that would mean delivering post around a much larger station and to be honest I really did not fancy that, so I declined. 'What about a job in the clerical and secretarial reserve in London then?' she asked. Without hesitation I said 'Yes.'

Transfer to London

I went home and told my parents that I would be off to London. 'Where are you going to live?' my mum asked with a frown and I suddenly realised that that would indeed be a problem.

'Don't worry Grant I'll telephone your Auntie Flo and see if she can put you up. Apparently Auntie Flo was delighted to put me up. She and my uncle Fred owned a transport café in Erith in South London not far from the railway station. Little did I know just how arduous a journey it was going to be from there to Broadcasting House in London. When the arrangements had been made for my transfer, Stella arranged a leaving party which was held in the small staff canteen and I was presented with a beautiful travelling leather case, which I still have today.

In truth, as I walked away from 36 Beechgrove Terrace for the last time as an employee I did feel a twinge of sadness as I had been treated so well by all of the staff working there during the three years I had worked there. So it was that on a wet Friday evening in January 1963 my father came with me to the railway station as I was taking the overnight train to Kings Cross in London. As he stood at the window he handed me an envelope. 'That will help get you started Grant, good luck,' he said and the train started its journey. Once I had settled down in the carriage I opened the envelope and was surprised that there was £25 in there, which was a lot of money back then.

I arrived at King's Cross station early the following morning around six-thirty, fairly tired, and looked at the instructions Auntie Flo had sent to my mum telling me what I should do to ensure that I arrived safely at her home, a flat above the transport café. First I had to find a tube train from Kings Cross to London Bridge then a British Rail train onto Erith Railway Station.

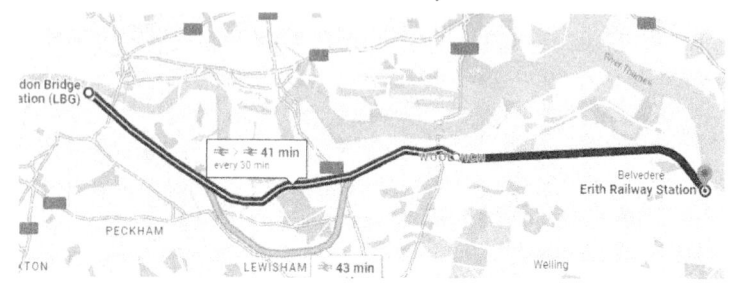

The café was only a five-minute walk away in Fraser Street. I made it okay but the journey took me an hour and twenty minutes. Auntie Flo could see that I was exhausted when I walked into the café in Fraser Street which was full of customers on a Saturday morning, so after a big hug and a few kisses on my cheek she took me to my room in the flat upstairs and told me to go to bed and have a rest, they would see me for lunch later. I saw Uncle Fred cooking some eggs and bacon in the largest frying pan I had ever seen as I passed by, he was a very big man indeed.

My aunt and uncle were very nice hard-working people who were up every morning at five thirty to prepare to open the café by 6am. Every morning when I arrived downstairs there was a huge breakfast waiting for me, two eggs, two thick bacon rashers, fried bread, fried tomato, and some mushrooms, plus two thick slices of toast and a steaming mug of tea. I had never in my life experienced such a large breakfast, but as I sat there trying to get it all inside me, lorry drivers, railway workers etc. were sat at other tables wolfing it all down in minutes, it was after all a transport café.

On the Monday morning at 7.20am I left the café and walked the short distance to Erith Railway station to catch the train to London Bridge and I was amazed at the amount of people waiting on the platform. When the train pulled in there was a mad scramble to get onboard and grab a seat, any seat.

I was not so lucky and I had to stand all the way to London Bridge where I changed onto the Northern Tube

Line and got off at Bank then onto the Central Line to Oxford Circus, the tubes were also very busy with commuters going to work. I can assure you it did not take me long to use my arms and body to ensure that I managed to get a seat on the train and the tube going to the BBC and coming back to the café after work.

The journey is of course much easier today.

I left Oxford Street Station and walked up Regent Street into Langham Place passing All Saul's Church, and in front of me was Broadcasting House. I stood and looked at the building with eight floors for several minutes then walked smartly across the road and a commissionaire opened one of the two large doors for me. The inside was impressive indeed with a huge ceiling and a large reception desk adjacent to two lifts.

Broadcasting House 1963

20

I approached the reception desk and said rather nervously, 'My name is Grant Bremner and I have been told to report here.' The female receptionist looked at a clipboard then said, 'You are a bit early, take a seat over there,' and she pointed to a long bench around one side of the curved wall. The large clock inside reception area informed me that the time was 8.45am and I was not due until 9.30am. I made a mental note that I could get up at least half an hour later during the weekdays.

I watched people come and go through the main doors while I waited and I was genuinely surprised just how many people there were, I assume the majority would be staff. Then I heard my name called and a female personnel officer walked over and introduced herself (sorry I don't recall her name). 'Grant you are now on the secretarial and clerical reserve and I note that you can type, yes?'

'Yes, I learned it in Aberdeen miss,' I replied quickly.

'Excellent, then follow me, I have a job for you in Bentinck House,' she said before she about-turned and strode off. I must admit that I was a bit surprised as I had expected to be working in Broadcasting House, nevertheless I did as I was instructed and followed her. It took less than five minutes to walk to Bolsover Street where Bentinck House was located. Here I was introduced to another female, a clerical supervisor who then took me to a desk where, yes, another Smith Corona typewriter was awaiting me, thankfully it was a slightly newer model. My instructions were to type from written sheets onto index cards ensuring that the headings were correct.

Bentinck House

There were a few other members of staff in the office, but I was not introduced to them. I set to my task with gusto and got quite a shock about an hour later when someone said loudly, 'Coffee break.' Immediately a number of staff left their desks and headed out of the building. 'Where are they off to?' I enquired, puzzled at their departure.

'They are off to the canteen at Broadcasting house, we have twenty minutes,' was the reply. 'Come with me and I'll show you.'

I believe her name was Martha, but can't be sure. However, we set off at a pace and were soon back at Broadcasting house, not through the main door but a much smaller one at the rear of the building. We wound our way along several corridors into a lift then up to the 8th floor, I believe, to the canteen that was almost full of staff members drinking and eating. To be honest by the time I had had a glass of milk it was time to rush back to Bentinck House making sure we did not go over the allocated twenty minutes.

I continued travelling from Erith to Bentinck House for several weeks then one day the supervisor informed me that there was a job they wanted me to do at the Maida Vale Studio (where the Dr Who theme was composed and produced later on). She told me I could claim for the tube fare, so off I set to Oxford Street Station onto the Bakerloo Line that would take me to Warwick Street Tube Station, the nearest station to Maida Vale Studios. I had been provided with written directions as to how to get to the studio that was located in Delaware Road.

BBC Maida Vale Studios

It was only when I arrived that I was informed that this was now my new place of work. My immediate thought was that I had now lost that extra half an hour in bed as this was now another tube train to take making it one train plus three separate tubes. I must admit I was not very happy at the prospect of the travelling and doubts entered my mind, had I made the correct decision in being transferred down to London from Aberdeen, even though I would have lost my job.

The next shock for me was when I was escorted down to the basement, going from a well-lit room with plenty of windows down some stairs then along a long narrow corridor and being shown into a basement room where there were literally thousands of master matrix twelve-inch disks stacked on shelves around this vast room. I immediately noticed the small desk containing yet another Smith Corona typewriter, the same model I had learnt to type on back in Aberdeen BBC. 'Your job, Grant, is to catalogue these disks with title, composer, and any other relevant information on the label. You may have noticed that we passed a coffee and tea machine in the corridor which you can use for your break.'

I just stood there open-mouthed looking at the enormous task ahead of me and felt a deep despair within me, was this to be my career in the BBC, stuck in a basement cataloguing all day and every day, I asked myself. Nevertheless, I buckled down to the job in hand in the belief that something better would soon come along, and by sheer chance it did about two months later.

I was summoned one day to an office and told to take a parcel to the Decca Recording studios in Finsbury Park and informed that I could claim the bus fares there and back. To this day I really don't understand why I did it but I said an emphatic, 'No, that's the job of a messenger, get one of them to take it,' and I walked back to the basement and continued typing. That same afternoon I had a visit from another female personnel office who simply informed me that I was expected the following morning to report to Egton House Sound Effects department. My immediate thought was that I could have that extra half hour sleep back.

Egton House

I really enjoyed working at Egton House where yet again I was set the task of cataloguing sound effects records, 78 rpm, along with the newer 45rpm ones. Jim Palm was the AIC (Assistant in Charge) and a really nice bloke to work for. He had a good sense of humour and he was not a hard task master either. There were about five other members of staff whose jobs were to answer the phone and give advice to production staff on what sound effects would be appropriate. Records were also dispatched twice daily to the Television Gramophone Library.

Above us was the main gramophone library where hundreds of thousands of recordings were kept and catalogued. It was the largest collection of records in the world. Later on in my career I was to become very familiar with both of these departments. However, my time was short lived as a member of staff had left Sound Archives in Broadcasting House so I was sent there after only one month.

My very first impression of Sound Archives was when I first walked in there and there was David Attenborough sat crossed legged on the floor going through a book catalogue of monkey sounds. By the way, I was now acting up another grade at SC3 and being paid for it also. Yes some cataloguing was required, but part of my new duties were to answer the telephone and advise whoever was calling on the appropriate recording they needed and arrange for their dispatch. The Librarian was a gentleman called Tony Trebble and he was a very interesting person with a great knowledge of what was contained within Sound Archives. He was approachable and would help me out on occasions when I was stuck for ideas. I was also to meet him later in life at Television Centre and we became good friends.

I had discovered that having been transferred from Aberdeen to London I was entitled to four travel vouchers within an eighteen month period to fly back to Aberdeen in order to see my family. I brought this up with personnel and I was told they would issue a train voucher. I shook my head and said that staff instructions stated that anyone living north of a line drawn through Perth would be entitled to travel by air. Of course this was checked by Miss Bratt who then rather grudgingly agreed that I was entitled to fly to Aberdeen and she made the necessary arrangements once I had given her the dates of my travel.

At this time, around September 1963, I took the decision to move from my aunt and uncle in Erith into the BBC Hostel in New Cavendish Street as a vacancy had occurred. To be completely honest I do not think they were disappointed at my move as it gave them more time to concentrate on the transport café they ran. Obviously much less travelling was involved as Broadcasting House was less than two minutes walk away from the hostel that was located in New Cavendish Street.

BBC Hostel New Cavendish Street

I was allocated a shared room on the first floor with David who worked at Bush House and we got on quite well, but certainly were not bosom buddies. We each had a small wardrobe and there was a wash basin too. I can't remember exactly how much I had to pay as it was taken out of my wages which were now being paid directly into my Barclay's bank account.

There was a small restaurant where you got a breakfast but you had to get your own lunch and dinner. There was also a table tennis room in the basement next to the washing machine and ironing area. The table was very close to one wall due to the placement of the door and over the months I became quite an expert at a backhand return that flew across the table. During my stay at the BBC hostel there was one particular incident that I will never forget.

One morning I woke up and found that I could not move my legs, I appeared to be paralysed. My room-mate David had already gone to work at Bush House, and I was only able to tap on the floor, but not very loudly, so no one heard me. Around 11 o'clock Sound Archives rang reception to ask if I was alright as I had not reported for duty. The manager came to my room and then called for the doctor, who sent for an ambulance. I was taken to Middlesex Training Hospital about a mile away.

Middlesex Training Hospital

At the time I thought I had polio which was prevalent at that time. A consultant examined me and surprisingly diagnosed tonsillitis even though I did not have a sore throat. Apparently the nerves at the rear of the throat were so swollen they were impacting on the spinal column affecting my ability to move my legs. As it was a teaching hospital he asked if it would be alright for student doctors to examine me and that he would operate the following Monday. I said yes, provided my work agreed. He telephoned the BBC who agreed. So, I spent a week being examined by a host of junior doctors and to the best of my knowledge no one diagnosed tonsillitis. After the operation on the Monday I did indeed have a sore throat but could again move my legs. The hospital was later demolished as it was not structurally sound and a new one was built.

On one particular day I arrived at work in Sound Archives wearing a polo neck jumper and within minutes I was summoned to the personnel office of a woman by the name of Ruth Bratt, apparently she had seen me enter the building. 'Grant you are supposed to wear a shirt and tie at Broadcasting House, polo necks will not do,' she said, rather testily as I recall.

'I'm afraid I can't afford to buy shirts on the salary I get,' I replied rather cheekily.

Without hesitation she opened a desk drawer and handed me a typed list of second-hand clothes shops near Soho. 'There you are, that should help,' she said looking at me directly.

'I was the youngest of three sons and wore enough hand-me-down clothes growing up. I don't intend to start that again,' I replied irritably.

'She shrugged her shoulders then said, 'Well I can give you twenty one-shilling vouchers to use in the canteen, that should get you a glass of milk and roll for a while.'

I picked up the vouchers but left the list of second-hand clothes shops on her desk and left her office. When I got back to my office they were horrified when I related the story of my interview to them, but then for the first time since starting work in Sound Archives I noticed that all the males were wearing a shirt and tie. Shortly after that incident the post I was acting up in an SC4 grade was advertised on a permanent basis, so obviously I applied with the expectation I would be appointed having been doing the job for some months. Two weeks later I was informed by letter that I had not been appointed. Angry and hurt that there had not even been an interview I hot-tailed it to Ruth Bratt's office to demand an explanation. She informed me with a big smile on her face that another individual had been on grade SC3 a couple of months longer than I, and therefore he had been appointed to the position ahead of me, even though I had been acting in the job. On leaving her office in an angry mood I stopped by one of the staff notice boards where various vacant posts were advertised throughout the BBC.

My attention was drawn to Returns Clerk Television Gramophone Library Grade SC4, so I immediately sat down and wrote my application then sent it off.

Two weeks passed by before I was informed that I had an interview at Television Centre with John Carter the AIC of the Gramophone Library in his office. At my interview he was accompanied by a personnel officer.

The first thing I noticed as I walked into reception at Television Centre in November was that people were wearing jeans, polo necks, open shirts, there was obviously no strict dress code here. The interview went well and I was informed that there was a backlog of two years of non-return gramophone records that would be the first priority. At the end of the interview I was shown the returns area and the rest of the Gramophone Library. I returned on the central line to Broadcasting House feeling I had done my best, now I had to wait.

An internal letter arrived for me one week later informing me I had been appointed and arrangements were being made for my transfer to Television Centre.

The Move to Television Centre

So it was in January 1965 that I entered Television Centre, the building that was going to be my place of work until 1988, apart from a couple of years in other jobs in different BBC premises.

Television Centre as it looked when I arrived in January 1965, five years after joining the BBC in Aberdeen.

Television Centre had seven large studios when I arrived, more were added later and there was always some large production on the go in each of them, including of course the news studios.

Studio 1: As can be seen from this photo, it was the fourth largest television studio in Britain at the time. It was 995 square meters (10,250 ft^2) and it opened on 15 April 1964.

Studio 2 was 223 square metres (2,400 ft^2). It opened in late 1960, it housed comedy programmes such as 'That was the Week That Was'. It was not initially converted to colour and closed in 1969, with the space being used as storage, but reopened in 1981.

Studio 3 was 594 square metres (6,390 ft^2) and opened on 29 June 1960. It was designed as a drama studio and had customised panels and fittings. The walls were slightly thicker to insulate it from noise from the Circle line and from the Hammersmith & City line (then still part of the Metropolitan line) of the London Underground. It was the first studio to be completed and was upgraded to colour in 1969.

Studio 4 was 585 square metres (6,300 ft^2) and opened in January 1961. TC4 was similar in design and layout to its neighbour, TC3. It was designed as a light entertainment studio and contained a rather unusual sound system called ambiophony. It was upgraded to colour in 1970.

Studio 5 was 223 square metres (2,400 ft^2) and opened in August 1961. It was used for the first half of its life by broadcasts from BBC Schools. There was an adjacent area used for schools programming that linked in with the studio. It was converted to colour around 1973, about the same time as schools broadcasts as a whole. TC5 hosted an experimental session in 1963 to create video 'howlaround' footage for 'Doctor Who', although only a small amount was used in the original title sequence as transmitted.

Studio 6 was 598 square metres (6,440 ft^2) opened in July 1967 to coincide with BBC Two's switch to colour. It was the first to be equipped with colour cameras. It was a strange design: it was originally designed to be split in two by a large removable wall, but this idea was abandoned.

Studio 7 was 223 square metres (2,400 ft^2) and opened in 1962, it was used for a variety of programmes and was home to children's programming such as *Going Live!*

Studio 8 was 602 square metres (6,480 ft^2) and opened in 1967. It was considered the best studio for television producers to use. It was the size that most programmes wanted and, based on the experience when building the other studios, was the best. It became the studio for comedy and sitcoms, because of its audience seating arrangements and size.

Television Centre was truly an amazing experience when, during coffee or lunch break, I would walk into the viewing galleries of each studio to see what productions were taking shape, especially the variety over the years I spent working there, along with approximately 8,000 other staff spread over several other BBC buildings.

Helios Fountain: In the centre of the main block was a statue of Helios, the Greek god of the sun, designed by T. B. Huxley-Jones to symbolise the radiation of television around the world. At the foot of the statue were two reclining figures, symbolising sound and vision, the components of television. It was originally a fountain but owing to the building's unique shape it was too noisy for the staff in the overlooking offices, and there were problems with water leakage into the videotape area which for a long time was directly beneath. Even though there was a foundation stone marked 'BBC 1956' in the basement of the main building, construction began in 1951 and Television Centre opened in 1960, the same year I joined the BBC in Aberdeen.

Television Gramophone Library

The Gramophone Library had seven staff including myself working there, all of whom had been there for several years. I was made very welcome and got down to work straight away. I must admit I was horrified when I began to open the stack of files that contained the details of the non-return records from production offices, producers, sound assistants and even secretaries, there were literally thousands of them and in no particular order. I set about putting them in date order first so I could tackle those records that had been outstanding for the past couple of years. Lost records were charged against the Music & Arts Department which the Gramophone Library was part of. I was determined to change that and have the productions or whoever had had them charged for the loss of such records and not have it come out of our budget, but that was to take me a couple of years before it was achieved. I made a lasting friendship with Melvyn Silverman who was an SC5 assistant who answered the phone and dealt with production enquiries helping them to choose appropriate music for their productions.

He was an expert in all kinds of mood music supplied by various companies in that particular field. It took me several months to get all of the records up to date and the library began to see the fruit of my labours as gramophone records slowly began to return to the library. Unfortunately I had to write off quite a few as lost, it being impossible to track down the individual who had *borrowed* them. By 1965 we were up to date and it was then clear that there was a tremendous number of records, including sound effects that had not been catalogued and therefore were unavailable for use. I had a meeting with John Carter and he agreed that overtime would be authorised if I, or anyone else in the library who could type, wanted to catalogue records. I mentioned it to the others but the only person who was interested was Melvyn.

Over the ensuing months we got to know each other very well as we usually did overtime from 17.30 to 20.00 every evening which certainly helped put extra money into our monthly wage. Melvyn told me that he was the secretary of TV1 branch of the ABS and he invited me to the Annual General meeting where to my astonishment I was elected as chairman at my very first meeting. This branch was the largest in Television Centre with close to 800 members as it covered all the clerical and secretarial staff, make-up artists, costume designers and dressers and wardrobe staff, plus a few other posts that did not belong to any other television branch, of which there were seven. TV2 was Video Tape, TV3 was a weekly paid branch, TV4 was production members, TV5 was engineering, sound and television cameramen, TV6 was weekly paid scenery staff and TV7 was a managerial branch.

Late in 1966 a vacancy occurred for an SC5 assistant in the Gramophone Library so obviously I applied and was successful. I now joined Melvyn Silverman, Jean Davis, Joan Lumley, Dorothy and Pam, and of course John Carter the AIC, as a library assistant and thoroughly enjoyed my new role.

As the months passed I became concerned that we were not given enough time to listen to the new records that were coming into the library on a daily basis, mainly classical recordings and mood music which was essential if we were to make recommendations to production staff for their programmes. This was not a decision that could be made by the AIC John Carter, so a meeting was held with the Administration Officer of Music and Arts, Ian Marshall, who took some persuasion, but eventually agreed that each assistant could have half a day a week to listen to new recordings.

I followed this request up by asking if we could have our own record players and a pair of good quality headphones by our desks. There were three listening rooms equipped with record players, tape decks and speakers but they were often in use by members of the productions teams or sound operatives, listening mostly to sound effect records. My request was granted and three weeks later our decks arrived with a decent pair of headphones.

36

Jimmy Saville was a frequent visitor to the Gramophone Library for records of artists that would be appearing on Top of the Pops every week. I have to say that it was well known that he was far too familiar with the young girls who had tickets for the show. They were often in his dressing room prior to and after the show had been recorded. In hindsight the BBC should have put a stop to this practice as they must have known what was going on.

Move out of the BBC Hostel

After about eighteen months of living in the BBC Hostel in Cavendish Street, now that I was working at Television Centre, I left the Hostel and rented a one room bedsit in Bayswater, but not for long as the owner's daughter took forever in the shared bathroom putting on her make-up. I then moved into a flat in Putney which I shared with Martin who also worked at the BBC at Bush House. I was soon to learn that he was absolutely useless as a cook and, as we could not afford to eat out or have take-aways other than the odd fish and chips, I did most of the cooking.

The Union - The ABS

On the union front, TV1 branch officers were always fairly busy throughout the next couple of years with a number of personal cases to be dealt with, plus various grading claims. One such grading claim related to the hours of work for the nurses working with the BBC

Doctor, Dr John Newman, in BBC Television Centre. I had held a meeting with the nurses who were unhappy about their long hours (they were not union members at the time) and I had informed them that the branch could only take this forward if they became members, which they were happy to do. The claim was submitted to the appropriate grading department and BBC Industrial Relations Department also got involved. It took several months with a number of meetings before the claim for a salary upgrade was upheld and their hours were adjusted downwards. They had been working 12-hour shifts, doing four days on and three days off. Now they were on a standard 8-hour shift and an extra nurse was engaged. This was a big success for TV1 branch.

Industrial action first took place in Television Centre in 1969 by the ABS. This was quickly seen as a new and alarming union militancy by the BBC management, since, although action had been bubbling away under the surface since at least 1965, it actually manifested itself on Saturday, October 11th, 1969.

In pursuance of a pay claim, and against the background of the ongoing talks on conditions of service, ABS members simply walked out without warning. In the studios, the effect was dramatic.

The ABS had notified the BBC it had intended to take twenty-four hour action, but had neither specified the form it would take, nor the precise date. It is difficult now to recognise the sense of shock felt by those affected, such industrial action had never taken place before. In one studio, senior Light Entertainment producer Yvonne Littlewood, could only console a tearful singer Petula Clark, after the crew members of TV5 did not return from dinner, leaving themselves, the orchestra, and the audience literally in the dark. The action was well supported where it counted, only 15 studio staff out of 220 on the rota had worked and the studios had virtually come to a standstill.

Relations with the ABS changed immediately as commented by Roger Chase, then Deputy Director of Television Personnel who said, 'It is impossible to exaggerate the significance of this strike to the whole television service, from top to bottom. What it represented, to the management, was the transformation of the ABS, it was when it dawned on us that it was obvious we now had an industrial union with some muscle.'

The industrial action continued for the next month in what was called a guerrilla action campaign by ABS members. The dispute had been sharpest in those areas where the workforce had industrial muscle, in Television Centre, and management was well aware that this would remain the case in future.

Director General Charles Curran told a Board of Management meeting at the end of the month that, as they had been and expected to be exposed in the television service, so it became essential to ensure that the conditions of service settlement when finally achieved was such as to meet the reasonable aspirations of Television Service staff, even if it meant that other Directorates had to suffer financially as a result. This was precisely what was to happen in the coming years as, to the growing frustration in BBC management in less powerful sections of the workforce and the ABS leadership, staff in areas close to production were able to extract favourable conditions for themselves. In the meantime, relations between the BBC and the ABS, which had historically been amicable – tended to get worse "in spite of everybody's best efforts, I mean nobody wanted it to get worse, but it tended to get worse" Roger Chase once told me during one of our many meetings over the ensuing years.

It must be understood that the BBC was changing, old working practices were gone, new technologies were coming on board, new working practices were required, irregular hours of work were required, and all of these changes were to be negotiated, not just accepted as in the past. Yes, Television Centre was a stronghold of the ABS and the Inter Branch Liaison Committee (IBLC) and it only got stronger during the ensuing years. I was to become its chairman in 1975, but more about that later.

Change of Career Direction

Back in the gramophone library my work carried on although the AIC John Carter became ill and was away from the department for nearly six months. Jean Davis was put in charge and I began to wonder if I should look for further opportunities perhaps within film department and in 1971 I applied for the post of a trainee film assistant at Ealing film Studios around the same time John Carter returned to the library. I often heard the sound of the Adagio for Spartacus by Aram Khachaturian coming from his office and we were all delighted to learn that his choice of music had been chosen for the opening and closing credits for the very popular and highly successful

Television Programme, The Onedin Line, that went on to run for 8 series with 91 episodes.

Front entrance BBC Film Studios Ealing

So off I went to start a new career direction at Ealing Film Studios. There were eight of us on the Film Assistant training programme that was to last a year and I am happy to say that I got on with everyone, including the instructors.

I had been there training for several months when the sad news came through that my old boss John Carter had died and that Jean Davis was going to be appointed as a Personnel Officer and a request was made to Film Department asking if I could be released from the training programme in order to return to take charge of the Gramophone Library.

The request was refused. I was never consulted and apparently it annoyed the Head of Film Assistants that the request had been made and from that day on relations with him were never the same. I was only informed about the request several months later when I met Jean Davis when I called in past Television Centre. I passed the course and was sent back to Projection in Television Centre but then was moved quickly to Kensington House to work on what were called Steinbeck machines.

Steinbeck Player & Editing Machine

The Steinbeck was a very clever editing and viewing machine that could take either 16mm or 35mm film and sound tape and I had become adept at their use in splicing both film and sound in sync. The man in charge of the four editing/viewing rooms was Gerry Beasley who was to become a firm friend. From him I learned a great deal about life in general and he taught me to stand up for myself.

One day a young Production Assistant dropped two cans of films by the door of the room I was working in, 'Take them back to film dispatch,' he said abruptly, then walked off. Gerry had overheard this comment, so without saying a word he found two stickers 'nitrate film – highly inflammable' and stuck them on the bottom of the two cans of film. 'Ring the production office Grant and tell them to come and shift these dangerous film cans and tell them to do it now.'

Now I could tell you the name of the Production Assistant concerned and those in the know will probably know the initials, so I rang the office and told AY to come back down and take the inflammable films back to film dispatch himself. He was down within the next couple of minutes and he took the film cans over to dispatch himself.

On another occasion a booking had been made for 2 o'clock in the afternoon to view a 35mm film, the infamous 'Deep Throat'. Well, another Production Assistant appeared at one forty-five when I was on my lunch break. He stuck his head around the door and demanded I put the film on there and then. Emboldened by the previous incident I told him politely that I was on my break and would load the film at the time it was booked. He went on to say he was in a hurry and told me again to load it now, I refused. He then went into the viewing room and tried to load the 35mm film on to the Steinbeck machine himself. The next thing I heard was the sound of film being torn as it was being fed through the machine having been incorrectly loaded. I rushed in and found that there was two hundred feet of film totally ruined. I made a report of the incident and we never saw that person back again. I also worked on the 'vox pops' of the That's Life programme on the recordings made with the public in the street. These were always late sessions on a Friday night as the 16mm film and sound tape had to be marked for editing for transmission the following evening. Sometimes finishing after midnight we'd be taken out for a meal. Of course Esther Rantzen was in attendance, but I'll remain silent on that.

In October '73 another Assistant post had become available in the Gramophone Library and as I had begun to realise that my chances of making it on to a Film Editor course were pretty slim given that the request from Music and Arts for me to return had not gone down well with Film Department, I decided to apply for my old post. By the end of the month I was back working in the Gramophone Library.

Jean Davis was gone, Joan Lumley was sharing the role of AIC with David Stone who had come over from the main Gramophone Library at Egton House. The main library was where we ordered our records from on a twice daily basis and it had an enormous collection of commercially-issued gramophone recordings covering both UK and overseas issues of the last 85 years, the present holdings being about 1,000,000, mainly discs (both coarse - and microgroove) also with some cylinders and cassettes. These were for BBC programme purposes only. They of course were not available to other organisations or members of the public.

I enjoyed being back working with Melvyn and of course having been a union member of the Ealing Film branch I was now back to being a member of TV1. Yes, you've probably guessed it by now, within two months I was back as Chairman of the branch with Melvyn still the secretary.

At Work in the Gramophone Library

I found working in the Gramophone Library very rewarding and it was good to be able to do something I knew I was good at. I enjoyed all genres of music from Pop and Country through to Jazz and Classical and I would often be given tickets from various production offices in Music & Arts to music events the BBC were covering, like the Proms at the Albert Hall for example.

BBC Club Television Centre

I was amazed at the size of the club at Television Centre, it was huge with two bars in separate rooms plus another room where you could buy a sandwich or have a salad. There was also an extensive outdoor seating area over the roof of Studio four where you could take your food and beverage whenever the weather would allow. I remember when I first went into the club in 1965, the first famous person I saw there was Andy Stewart the Scottish singer and entertainer who had hits with A Scottish Soldier and

Donald Where's Your Troosers? Many artists would come there to relax after a show along with members of the production staff.

There was also a booth where you could buy cigarettes (they were allowed back then) and bottles of alcohol like Whisky, Gin etc. The lady who was in charge of the booth was a very friendly lady called Gladys, and she was well known to those who patronised the club.

A gift from Gladys, a set of table mats

I would often go to meet other union members to have a relaxing drink and discuss union matters. I doubt many other large employers would have licensed bars on their premises that staff could use freely. There were of course many other Club activities one could join - tennis, cricket, football, plus so many more.

ABS TV1 Branch

I was most fortunate indeed to have such an abundance of talent on the branch committee. Melvyn Silverman was an excellent secretary of the committee, his desk was always littered with files and papers but when you asked for one of them he put his hands on it immediately.

Prue Handley, a Senior Costume Designer, was a member for many years who became chairman when I moved on. She had a keen and sharp mind and was no fool when it came to discussions with the management, we have remained friends until this day. Jean Steward, a Make-up artist, also served on the committee for many years and her input during their grading dispute was instrumental in the award that was achieved. Roy Davis was a Back Projectionist who was another stalwart of the committee, he took over as chairman after I had moved on to the Managerial Branch TV7. Lorraine Dance was also an excellent committee member who had a clever insight into the inner workings of BBC management and she did not suffer fools gladly. I put all successes of the branch, of which there were many, down to those individuals and many more members who served on the committee and who worked so hard on behalf of the members for many years.

Over the years I was amazed at the commitment put in by committee members, attending lengthy meetings often out of working hours. Their ability to grasp complex problems when required plus their debating skills in front of an intimidating management was inspiring at the very least. I knew that I could always rely on the committee members to back me up during negotiations, something of which the management was also well aware.

The branch continued to attract new members, not only because of its success but also staff were beginning to realise that if they wanted help with either a personal case or conditions of service then being a union member could only help.

To be perfectly honest I was often surprised by just how much notice the BBC Television management took of the union and I soon saw that in certain circumstances there was genuine sympathy for some of the problems we were raising on behalf of our members.

It was noticeable that instead of dealing and negotiating with managers it was personnel officers who were taking the lead and making decisions affecting members of staff which then the managers had no option but to go along with whether they agreed with the conclusions or not. The old days when staff were expected to do anything they were told, were dead and buried for the foreseeable future, until of course the power of the unions nationally was greatly diminished by Maggie Thatcher and her lot. However, for now the unions, particularly the ABS within Television, had a great deal of bargaining power and we used it to the full.

Workings of TV1 Branch:

The following was taken from 'Broadcast', the ABS magazine, in 1974 that gives a good example of the work undertaken by the branch committee.

Branches

London Television No 1

The Deputy General Secretary and the Editor of *Broadcast* were present from Head Office at the Annual General Meeting of the London Television No. 1 branch held at Television Centre on Monday, 18 November.

The branch officers, who were present, were Grant Bremner (Chairman), Jean Steward (Vice-chairman), Melvyn Silverman (Secretary), Rose Hickarda (Assistant Secretary) and Avril Stewart (Records Secretary).

Below is the text of the joint report of the Chairman and the Secretary.

Introduction

In trying to assess the work of the Branch Committee over the past year, TV1 members should take into account some of the difficulties the committee has been faced with over the year.

This has been one of our worst years regarding our relationship with management. During the earlier part of the year there was the dispute involving the show working operatives. Then during the summer, there was the PA strike lasting over seven weeks. These two disputes also showed us the solidarity that our members have when one section of staff has a legitimate grievance.

TV1 Branch is now the largest in the ABAS and covers a great many people working in different departments throughout television. One problem that arises from a large branch such as ours is that of communications. We have striven to inform all our members of all union activities but we have experienced problems and I would hope that the new branch committee will look into the problems of communications. I would at this stage remind all our members of the official union notice boards in most buildings and that all committee members can usually be contacted by telephone.

We have been most fortunate in having Officers from Head Office attending our General Meetings and at normal Committee Meetings as well and I would hope that this practice will continue next year.

I would, on behalf of the Committee, like to thank the secretary of the branch for his outstanding work during the past year.

Committee

The Committee elected at last year's AGM, consisted of 20 members. During the year we had three resignations and these vacancies were filled at a general meeting held in April at which an election took place. The committee also co-opted a further two members during the year. These were Miss K. Carswell (Make-Up) and Miss V. Fryer (Network Assistant), as it was felt that we particularly required representatives from these areas.

During the year the committee has had a very heavy volume of business to deal with, much of it complicated in nature and covering many departments. We have always tried to process this work as rapidly as possible but, with a large amount of grading claims ranging from one dealing with a single member to another covering 150 members, there have been some unfortunate delays. We have been very concerned at the length of time some claims have taken but have always striven to meet deadlines set by management. However this has not always been the case on management's part, especially when dealing with the grading claim of the producers' assistants.

The committee has been very concerned by the non-attendance of certain members throughout the year. To try and solve this problem we shall be asking the AGM to approve an amendment to the standing orders of the branch committee effectively to deal with this problem.

Meetings
The committee has met on a monthly basis with meetings lasting up to three hours. The attendance has been slightly better than last year but still needs to improve.

During the PA strike we held weekly meetings to enable us to keep up with the latest developments and to inform the membership. At the first of these meetings a resolution was passed asking the NEC to set up a strike fund. On behalf of the committee I would like to thank all of our members who gave generously to this fund.

General Meetings
There have been five general meetings during the year. Two of them to discuss the PA dispute, and to endorse the committee's support for the PAs. The second of these meetings was attended by 75 of our members.

Apart from the two meetings on Annual Council, a special meeting was held in September to discuss the committee's decision to support the calling of a Special Council to discuss the recent pay settlement. Although the attendance was poor, it was a very lively meeting, with the committee receiving endorsement of its decision.

A special meeting was held at Kensington House for members in that area, and as a result, a small sub-committee has been established in this area to discuss problems that they have. To date this sub-committee has held three useful meetings at which AGS Nick Bunyan was present.

A number of meetings have been held with the producers' assistants regarding their grading claim. A sub-committee was set up at the second meeting to deal with the background of the claim and to meet with management.

Membership
The branch membership now stands at 831 which is an improvement and we feel general recognition that staff are beginning to see that the only way to improve their working conditions is to join an effective union.

A number of recruitment meetings have also been held, and although we have increased our membership, we are still well down on recruitment of the secretarial and clerical staff.

Personal Cases
Unfortunately, the number of personal cases has continued to increase. The committee had its resolution on personal cases passed at Annual Council and the NEC has now set up a sub-committee to look at the personal record and annual reporting systems, as used by the BBC, with the ultimate aim of improving these systems. The committee hopes for progress in this area.

ABS Activities
The branch through its nominated representative has been represented at the London Television Inter Branch Liaison Committee meetings (IBLC), which deals with problems common to all branches in that area, e.g. co-productions, outside hire, security, development of miniaturised cameras, etc.

Local Liaison
So far this year, the committee has been able to arrange for a further two departments to have local liaison meetings, these being Costume and PABX. At present, discussion is taking place for a further two departments. The whole question of local liaison meeting for TV1 is under consideration by the committee as management have sent us proposals covering all areas of TV1. We would hope to report on these proposals at a later date.

Annual Council
The branch Committee submitted three resolutions, the first being to alter the name of the ABS. (This was defeated). The second was on personal records, as previously mentioned. The third requested that members only attended Council. (This was also defeated.)

The Committee nominated the Chairman for the NEC and four nominations for the Advisory Panels. All of our nominees were elected.

Special Council
Mention has already been made of the Committee's decision to support the call for a Special Council. Although this was not the type of Council we were hoping for (no resolutions were allowed under rule). The branch sent seven delegates. A number of branches with members in the OP structure were dissatisfied with the pay settlement but not enough to reject the NEC's report.

SI 321
The committee has been trying to exert pressure on the NEC to re-negotiate SI 321 to remove some of the anomalies in this staff instruction which penalises some of our members.

Schedule A and Meal Allowances
We have once more rejected the offer that was put forward it was felt that they were totally unrealistic in keeping abreast with today's prices, although an improved offer was finally accepted, the committee feels that it is still unsatisfactory.

Future of Broadcasting
The Committee requested the NEC to allow branches the publication *People and the Media*. This request was

refused. The Committee felt that urgent attention should be given to the views of the membership as a whole regarding the future of broadcasting. We would ask any member with views on this important subject to contact any member of the committee.

MP Conditions of Service

There has been concern in two areas on the new MP conditions of service. A meeting was held with members and DGS P. Leech at which the present problems were discussed. It is hoped to negotiate locally on these problems.

The members of the 1974 Committee were: Miss S. Carter, Mrs. S. Channing-Williams, M. Catherwood, D. Coles, H. Coventry, P. B. Day, Miss J. Hagger, Miss R. Landau, Miss M. Pratt, Miss A. Paul, Miss K. Pearce, K. Sharp, A. B. Snoaden, Miss F. Sturt, Mrs. P. Wall, Miss K. Carswell and Miss V. Fryer (Co-opted Members).

From this fairly lengthy article you will get an idea of just how much work the TV1 branch committee were undertaking on behalf of such a diverse branch with 813 members.

Other Unions representing BBC Staff

It may be useful to know a little bit of the history of the ABS (Association of Broadcasting Staff) which was recognised across all areas by the BBC. Other unions obtained recognition over the years for certain occupations:

The NUJ (National Union of Journalists) in news; NATTKE (National Association of Theatrical Television and Kine Employees) mainly in the scenery department; and of course the EETPU (Electrical, Electronic, Telecommunications and Plumbing Union) organised some of the electricians although not that many. Some

ABS members were also members of other recognised, or in some cases, unrecognised unions such as the ACTT (Association of Cinematograph Television and Allied Technicians), which represented technicians in the commercial sector.

There was no closed shop agreement with the BBC, which to an extent weakened the ABS, and it never enjoyed the same leverage with management as its counterparts in commercial television. Twice, in 1968 and again in 1975, the ABS via Tony Hearn had tried unsuccessfully to persuade the BBC to allow a closed shop with it in order to resist encroachments from the ACTT, but the corporation had refused, viewing a closed-shop as incompatible with editorial freedom, and had told the unions that, on this, they were prepared to go off air for an indefinite period rather than concede. The BBC Staff Association was founded in 1945 becoming the Association of Broadcasting Staff in 1956 finally affiliating to the Trades Union Congress (TUC) in 1963. Then in 1974, it expanded further becoming the Association of Broadcasting and Allied Staffs.

In 1978 there was a move to amalgamate with the ACTT to become AFBU (Amalgamated Film and Broadcasting Union). Voting in August 1978 the members of both unions voted in favour of amalgamation and application to secure the registration of the instrument of amalgamation by the Certification Officer was made. However, in March 1979 the Certification Officer said that he would not register the instrument of amalgamation until the ACTT had conducted a further ballot. In the end, amalgamation between the ACTT and the ABS never happened.

An amalgamation did take place in 1984, but this was between the ABS and NATTKE (National Association of Theatrical Television and Kine Employees), the amalgamated union becoming BETA (Broadcasting and Entertainment Trades Alliance).

Note: In 1991 (after my time) there was a further amalgamation when BETA and ACTT merged becoming BECTU (Broadcasting, Entertainment, Cinematograph and Theatre Union).

Conditions of Service

In the 70s a number of disputes occurred within Television Centre mainly over 'conditions of service' which had been negotiated in the late 60s over a two-year period by Tony Hearn and the BBC.

I went out of my way to study this fairly lengthy document and it became my foremost reference point during many disputes and grading claims. Unintentionally these conditions of service created various disparities between different groups of workers, some of whom qualified for the new enhanced payments and some of whom did not. Supervisors and managers who were on MP grades did not receive overtime payments for example as they often earned less than the staff they supervised. It was even suggested by some managers that the conditions of service should be renegotiated by Leslie Page, the then Controller of Personnel in television, however he considered this 'not a practical proposal to put to the union.' It was also clear that the ABS's power base lay in the OP grades (Operational) who had benefitted to some extent from these arrangements.

The following is an extract from a Tony Hearn interview: 'There's no doubt [...] because I thought so at the time, that we over-played our hand in some of those disputes in the 70s [...] we pushed the BBC too far. I used to try and convince our executive of that but keeping the militants, in inverted commas, in check was very difficult [...]. So you see there were these tensions within the union. We had to give a bit and we couldn't keep a curb on the television branches as much as we might have. All things being equal and that meant we were being dragged by the television branches into disputes that the BBC obviously didn't want us to win.'

This was a view to which neither I nor the TV branches' members, or even some officials, would have subscribed. As chairman of TV1 branch I instigated several grading claims on behalf of several groups of staff, in particular Make-up Artists, who in comparison to their ITV counterparts were badly paid. The BBC was excellent in their training programmes and it took a Make-up Artist seven years to become fully qualified. Then as soon as they were, it was quite common for ITV to poach them by offering much higher salaries. In my view management should have recognised this but after several meetings with them it was clear that they were not prepared to budge. By this refusal TV1 was able to recruit almost the complete workforce in furtherance of their claim. Their local representative was Jean Steward who was an excellent asset during our meetings with Hans Norton from BBC Industrial Relations Manager who just could not keep his eyes off the very lovely Jean. The claim was eventually successful and the Make-up members were of course very pleased with the outcome.

Television IBLC (Inter-branch Liaison Committee)

By 1973 I was elected Vice-Chairman of the Television IBLC (Inter-branch Liaison Committee) and in 1976 was elected Chairman, when John Elfes became Chairman of the ABS. At my first meeting with Leslie Page, Controller of Personnel, and his team of managers, under 'Any Other Business' I stated that I was concerned regarding certain questions that were being asked of candidates at interviews. I went on to say that in my opinion there were three areas that should never be mentioned - their religion, their sex, and definitely not whether or not they were a union member. Even I, as well as the other BBC managers present, was amazed when he replied without hesitation, 'I agree completely, it will be done.' I saw that as my real success but it came at a price as some of the BBC personnel at that meeting never forgot it or me.

Workings of the TV IBLC:

Television IBLC

Grant Bremner was elected chairman for the remainder of the year when the Television IBLC met on 19 May. Chick Anthony (London TV5) was confirmed as vice-chairman for the remainder of the year.

At the outset, the meeting recorded a vote of thanks to John Elfes for his past service to the IBLC as chairman and member and conveyed its best wishes to him in his future work as Chairman of the Association.

At the meeting were representatives of London TV1 – 7 branches, London TV News, Ealing Film Operations, Acton 1 and 2 branches and Alexandra Palace, together with NEC Rapporteur Reg Hutchings, AGS Celia Croasdell and ABS Chairman John Elfes.

The major items on the agenda were cuts in television production, technical developments, the "Multi-Colour Swap Shop" and reports on meetings with the television management.

BBC Finances – Television

Reports on the latest meetings with the management were presented and it was noted that the Deputy General Secretary was having discussions with the management in which he had put forward the Association's policy on the use of outside hire and contract labour. It was noted that the television management had undertaken to provide full information at local level on the vacancies which were being frozen and to differentiate between those which were vacant due to the economies and those which were vacant for operational reasons.

The Committee emphasised that branches should ensure that full discussions were taking place at local level on all posts held vacant and that the outcome of all such discussions should be reported to the officer so that information could be collated at the IBLC level.

Programme Planning

A report which had been sent to the NEC was presented and discussed and it was noted that further clarification of the figures and retrospective information on all programmes produced in London television, broken down by departments, was being sought from the management.

Security

It was noted that the question of the alleged boycott of security by BBC staff working in the News area had been discussed with the management which was looking into the complaint. The IBLC reiterated its major concern that there should be adequate backing for commissionaires and that this be conveyed to the London TV3 branch and to the management.

Technical Development Sub-Committee

The summer peak staffing arrangements produced by the management in April were discussed and accepted in principle by the IBLC. However, it was felt that progress on the wider issue of the studio, film and OB exchange attachment scheme was not considered satisfactory and the IBLC saw no reason why the management should not proceed immediately with the setting up of a camera exchange attachment scheme and the implementation of longer term attachments on the sound side.

It was also noted that meetings had been held with the management to discuss proposals for an electronic news gathering experiment. Concern was expressed about the future of technical operators working with electronic equipment outside the News area although it was pointed out that the future for members employed in film could cause equal concern.

The consensus of opinion was that the IBLC should impress on the management the need for adequate training facilities and proper recruitment policies to ensure that the detrimental effects on staff of technological developments are kept to the absolute minimum.

Management Liaison

AGS Celia Croasdell reported on meetings with the television management and drew attention particularly to discussions on stereo, the Olympic Games and the Ealing agreement on cutting rooms.

"Multi-Colour Swap Shop"

A report was presented on discussions which had taken place with the management about the conditions of service applicable to staff working on the "Multi-Colour Swap Shop". It was noted that the management had now offered a schedule which qualified all operational staff for a half-night shift payment. The IBLC recommended formally to the NEC that the management's latest proposal be accepted on condition that all members required to report for duty before 08.00 hours do so on a volunteer basis. (The IBLC's recommendation was discussed at length at the NEC's meeting held on 27 May. The NEC instructed that the management's latest proposals be accepted).

National Executive Committee

At the annual conference of the union in 1974 I was elected onto the National Executive Committee and at its first meeting I was elected onto the Admin & Finance Committee becoming chairman in 1976, a position I held until 1982. Reg Hutchings from TV5 was then the President of the ABS and he chaired the meeting of the National Executive Committee. Executive meetings were held every month in ABS Head Office which was in Goodge Street in Central London.

ABS Offices in Goodge Street

I was going to spend a good deal of my time there over the ensuing years.

I must admit that I was rather surprised to be elected onto the National Executive Committee the first time I put myself up for election. My father was a union man and was very proud of my union activities.

Grant Bremner, London TV1 Branch, was elected at Council to serve on the NEC for the coming year.

Administration & Finance Committee:

There were five members of the executive on the committee including the chairman and Jack Rogers, the Administration and Finance Officer. I firmly believed that it was our responsibility to look after the finances of the union and ensure that the members' subscription money was being used in a prudent and correct manner. It was a very responsible committee as its main function was to look after the finances of the union which of course all came from the subscriptions paid by our members. Sadly, I soon discovered this was not the case as money was being frittered away in a number of ways that I thought required strict action. We checked members travel claim expenses for those delegates who came to a meeting from branches across the country and of course they were paid any overnight expenses they might incur. Unfortunately some members would travel back to their home on the same day/evening but claim for an overnight stay and apparently no one had bothered to ask for a receipt for their accommodation.

Jack Rogers, the ABS's Admin & Finance officer, was a likeable man with a warm personality, but he did not like to question anyone regarding their claims. When I became Chairman in 1976 I instigated a new system that required proof of overnight expenses and although there were a few grumbles from the membership, we began to save some money. Of course having applied this to the members of the ABS the same rule then applied to the officers working for the union of which there were eight plus the General Secretary Tony Hearn.

I was also amazed to see just how high the ABS hospitality account was running, and I was determined to do something about this, it was the members' money after all is said and done. It took a couple of years, but in the end it came down to an acceptable amount.

General Secretary Tony Hearn:
There is absolutely no doubt whatsoever that Tony Hearn was a gifted man with a first-class memory. He joined the union at the age of 26 as an assistant to the then

General Secretary Leslie Littlewood in 1955. He later became Deputy General Secretary and in 1972 he became the General Secretary of the ABS. He took a two-year break when he attended Oxford University and returned in time to complete the negotiations with the BBC on the Conditions of Service. It was well known that Tony liked his wine, a lot of wine and, on many occasions after imbibing too much, he would have a taxi ordered to take him back to his home just outside Oxford.

I first noticed this when a bill for over £2,000 from the taxi company arrived. It was brought up at the A&F committee and the decision was taken to confront the General Secretary regarding this unauthorised expenditure.

Jack Rogers and Eric Stoves both said they would come to support me, however at the appointed day and time neither showed up. I met Tony alone, gave him the bill and said the A&F committee would not authorise payment for this as, on the dates in question there had been no meetings. I told him that he would have to pay the bill himself. He was not a happy man and the meeting got testy. I told him that I would authorise the bill but that we would deduct a sum of money from his monthly salary until the bill was paid. This he eventually reluctantly agreed to.

There was one incident a couple of years later in the BBC Club bar at Television Centre. Tony had been meeting with Roger Chase, Head of Personnel, and had obviously enjoyed a few glasses and had then gone to the BBC club to continue drinking. Luckily I happened to go into the club bar around eight o'clock to find a drunk General Secretary arguing noisily with a Production Assistant member, Graham Benson, who had recently been on strike. It was clear to me that I had to get Tony away from the situation so I grabbed him and took him down to reception where I called the same taxi company to come and take him home. When the taxi arrived (Leinster Cars I believe) I informed the driver of Tony's condition, to which he replied, 'I've taken him home often enough in the past and know the situation well.' I stood there thinking how ironic it was that I was the person who had stopped him using taxis to get home and now I was ordering one, but then I reasoned the circumstances were different that evening as he had been at Television Centre to attend a meeting.

The Bet: One day in the summer of 1978 I left Television Centre and travelled to Goodge Street to have a meeting with Tony.

When I arrived around five o'clock I eventually found him in a room called the 'think tank' with our solicitor John Williams and Alan Jones, the Editor of the union magazine. All already appeared to me to have made good use of the hospitality cabinet. Annoyed that Tony was in no condition to have a meeting with me, I told him that he should stop drinking so much and then said 'I bet you can't stay off the booze for 3 months'. Instantly he responded, 'put your money where your mouth is Bremner.' To which I said, 'fifty pounds on it.' Tony leant forward and we shook hands. News of the bet quickly spread around the executive committee and I was congratulated by the Chairman Eric Stoves and a few others who said they'd chip some cash in if I had to pay the bet. Fifty pounds was a lot of money in those days.

£50 bet

I am pleased to say that I lost the bet and Tony Hearn managed to stop drinking alcohol not only for those three months but for the following four years. I was delighted that I'd lost the bet, but needless to say, no one on the executive helped me with the money I'd lost!

Meetings in Pubs:

Another incident occurred with the Deputy General Secretary Paddy Leech who used to submit expense claims for meetings outside office hours. These expense claims were usually submitted late and with no specific dates.

I informed the executive committee that the A & F committee required specific dates for all claims and they must be submitted at the latest on a monthly basis. Paddy's expense claims were usually three months late so difficult to check. Although he been present at the executive meeting when late claims had been discussed his next claim was again almost three months late with no specific details although there were some dates. In checking back I was able to ascertain that no meeting that had taken place at Head Office had gone on after five-thirty. It goes without saying that ABS members also used to go to the local pubs to talk about union matters and relax.

So, a meeting was arranged with Paddy and I was to be accompanied by Jack Rogers the Admin officer who once again failed to show for work. I met with Paddy myself and informed him that I could not authorise this latest claim as no meetings had taken place in the evening. His response was, 'I was meeting with the members in the Valiant Trooper or the (unknown Pub Name about 100 yards away) and I am entitled to claim expenses for that.' I pointed out that several meetings had concluded by three in the afternoon and all delegates had gone home. Paddy was not a happy man but his claims in future were accurate and submitted on time.

The Valiant Trooper Pub

Time-Off for Union Duties

The Television Directorate was generous with the paid time off they gave to Branch Officials and local union representatives. Melvyn Silverman as secretary and I as Chairman of TV1 branch were allowed time off to attend branch meetings and, of course, meetings with management, of which there were many. This arrangement meant that the Gramophone Library was often two members of staff down, so I held a meeting with the new Controller of Television Personnel, Roger Chase, and his assistant Gary Richmond to discuss the problem. It was quickly agreed that the Gramophone Library would have an extra assistant on a permanent basis to help with the workload.

I had by now been appointed to the position of AIC Television Gramophone Library following the departure of David Stone and Maureen Broderick who left the BBC to establish their own mood music company. Of course there was an interview as several other candidates had applied. Ian Marshall from Music & Arts telephoned me late that afternoon to inform me that I been appointed to the post.

I spent as much time as I could in the Gramophone Library as I thought my staff should see me as much as possible. However, when I became Chairman of the Television IBLC in 1976 and continued as Chairman of TV1, I spent a lot of time on Union duties. This was made much worse as during this period it became known by the union members in Television Centre that I could be contacted in the Gramophone Library and a number of members did so. In particular there was a dispute between the Scenic Artists (who were members of TV1

Branch) and the painters (who were members of another union NATTKE). Two Scenic Artists in particular, George Thain & Fred Tate, would come to my office two to three times a week over what I saw as a trivial matter that their manager could have sorted easily had they bothered to ask. However, they had to seek my advice first. It soon became clear that due to my ongoing commitments for the union, as chairman of TV1, Chairman of the Television IBLC (Inter-branch Liaison Committee), Executive member, and Chairman of the A&F committee, my union activities left me little time to fulfil my position as AIC of the Gramophone Library, so Roger Chase agreed that Melvyn, my deputy in the Gramophone Library, would act up in my capacity and be paid accordingly, allowing me to have fully paid time off from my BBC job to fulfil all my union commitments. This continued until 1984 when I relinquished the role of Chairman of the IBLC.

It was then that Roger Chase became the key figure in the BBC's industrial relations and the major architect of the modernisation of its personnel policies.

He believed firmly in union representation and often used the 'art of adjournment' to give all sides an opportunity to rethink. In 1982, Roger was asked to undertake the new role of deputy director of Personnel and, in 1989 joined the Board of Management, the first director of Personnel appointed from within. He was a man for whom I had a tremendous respect as he had for me.

We enjoyed over the ensuing years a good working relationship albeit on opposite sides of the table, and we never really fell out as each understood the other's position. We even had an occasional meal and drink together well away from Television Centre when no union or management business was discussed.

I would of course occasionally pop into the Gramophone Library to keep abreast of the new music and do some work too, especially when Melvyn was on annual leave. It was my safe haven (apart from the Scenic Artists popping in) where I was able to put union matters behind me albeit for a short period of time.

When the programme, I Claudius, was being recorded in Studio 1 during 1976, the word on the grapevine was it was well worth a visit to the viewing gallery as there were nude scenes being recorded. Melvyn and I decided to go and have a look to see if the rumours were correct, but our plans were thwarted by two commissionaires who had been stationed outside the viewing gallery in order to stop staff like us hoping to see what was going on down on the studio floor.

Union Office at Television Centre:

In 1977 the ABS was allowed to open an office on the ground floor of a prefabricated two story building adjacent to the main entrance of Television Centre. This was due to the amount of work that not only I was undertaking but also the other union representatives within Television Centre. Following a request from me, ABS head office decided to employ a secretary for the new Television office. Her name was Vivian Bellman and she was an excellent secretary indeed and very trustworthy. We got on very well during the years we worked together.

Me in the ABS office Television Centre

I spent a great deal of time working in the ABS office as Chairman of the Television IBLC given that I had been granted full time off from my BBC duties.

In the photo below the building to the left is where the ABS office was located.

Here I am asking an employee outside Television Centre to sign a petition.

Car Parking Facility: As I was often called to other BBC buildings for meetings with management or union representatives I was finding it impossible to park the car as there was limited space available for car parking on the main site. When I was on my motorbike, I had no problem as I was able to park it adjacent to our own union office at Television Centre. I raised the problem with Gary Richmond, Assistant to Roger Chase, and lo and behold I was issued with a car park sticker for the central car park right next to the entrance to Television centre.

This used to be a car park for senior managers.

You should have seen the look on the faces of some of the managers who also parked there when they saw me come and go as I pleased. A number of them made a formal complaint to Roger Chase, but it fell on deaf ears.

Other Personnel Officers in Television:

From 1974 onwards I came into contact with a number of different Television Personnel Officers as they were always present as part of the management team when either informal or formal discussions were required and when negotiations took place, of which there were many. Dick Craig was the Personnel Officer for Television Engineering who, as I write this, is 101 years old and a close friend with whom I have kept in touch after leaving the BBC on health grounds. Dick was given the responsibility to negotiate the introduction of Breakfast Television, as was I. Tony Hearn for reasons of his own decided not to attend, more on this later. Roger Johnson was another Personnel Officer who was responsible for the Film Editors within Television and another man who I respected as he did me. Tony Trebble was another Personnel Officer with whom I had a good working relationship over the years. Steve Ansell had come down from Glasgow and his area of responsibility was Central Services which included PABX, we also became good friends. There were of course many others, but too many to mention and meetings with them were not on such a regular basis.

My own Personnel Officer for Administration & Secretarial Staff in Television was Dick Gray (not be confused with Dick Craig). He was totally different, friendly on the surface, but ready to do management's bidding when required. Then there was Duncan Thomas, Head of Scenic & Design Group, who had recently come down from BBC Glasgow. To say that he and I did not get on would be at best an understatement as I genuinely believe that the man hated me, and I certainly did not like him. He detested with a vigour any victory the union achieved even though it may have benefitted the staff he was responsible for. I had numerous meetings with him present, and I always felt he resented me being there. That said, I consider myself fortunate to have come across so many nice people throughout my career within the union and BBC management, however there is always one bad apple lurking about.

Personal Note: On a personal level I must mention that in February 1974 the ABS officer responsible for TV1 was Nick Bunyan and of course I had reason to speak to him on a regular basis on union business. The only trouble was that Nick was a difficult man to track down as he was often out of his office on other union business, or he just didn't want to speak to me. Therefore, I spent a lot of time talking to his secretary, Sue Radley, and I do believe that I fell in love with her voice over the telephone. She was charming, easy to talk to and we appeared to get on well on the phone. Then a few months later I was due to attend a meeting at Head Office so I asked her if she would like to go out for a drink that evening, she agreed. We met in the Valiant Trooper and I knew then that she was without doubt the person that I would love all my life. We did eventually get married and have been exceedingly happy together throughout the years.

ABS Meetings

Special Meetings:

Being a member of the National Executive Committee often meant attending other meetings.

The ABS organised many such special meetings.

Celia Croasdell
Members ask BBC to "think again" about OU move to Milton Keynes. Open University members remain unconvinced

The Editor and I attended a meeting on 14 June at Alexandra Palace to discuss the proposed move of Open University production facilities to Milton Keynes. This had been arranged by the Alexandra Palace branch committee and the London TV4 Alexandra Palace members, all ABS members at the Palace were invited to attend. The chairman of the Television IBLC, Grant Bremner, chaired the meeting

BROADCAST JULY/AUGUST 1976

Left to right: John Moss, Dave Willson (AP), Grant Bremner (Chairman), AGS Celia Croasdell.

BROADCAST JULY/AUGUST 1976

Left to right:
Grant Bremner
(Television IBLC),
Richard Callanan
(London TV4),
Dave Willson
(Alexandra Palace),
John Moss
(Alexandra Palace).

The healthy attendance at the meeting, as well as being heartening to those invited from Head Office, clearly demonstrated the interest and concern which ABS members at Alexandra Palace have in the future of Open University productions. Council has shown that they have the support of their colleagues. Now we must go on to convince the BBC management, the Open University and, ultimately, the Government.

It was important for ABS head office to ascertain the views of the membership across the board, which would on occasion require delegates from all parts of the United Kingdom to be invited to attend, dependent on the subject matter at hand. Special halls had to be hired that were capable of housing upwards of 200 union representatives. A professional company was usually hired to supply the sound and recording equipment.

It was Jack Rogers with the help of John Rickards who organised the venues where the union representatives would meet and he always did his utmost to get these venues at as cheap a rate as possible. Often they had to be arranged at short notice especially when members were on strike and it was quite usual for a theatre or a cinema to be booked in order to accommodate up to two thousand members.

Special Councils:

Over the years I attended many special councils similar to the one below.

Special Council Ratifies Association's Response To Annan Committee Report

A total of 150 delegates from 84 branches of the Association attended the one-day Special Council held at the Cavendish Conference Centre in London on Saturday, 18 June.

The Special Council, to debate the Association's attitude and response to the report of the Committee on the Future of Broadcasting (the Annan Committee) had been called as a result of a resolution passed at this year's Annual Council.

The debate was based on a draft submission prepared by the National Executive Committee and circulated some two weeks in advance by the Special Council to all branches. The NEC's submission itself took into account the comments and advice sent to it by branches and by inter-branch liaison committees.

The Association's formal submission to the Home Secretary (as published in this issue) is based on the NEC's draft paper as modified by emergency propositions passed at the Special Council.

Some difficulty was experienced in co-ordinating all views because of the 1 July deadline set by the Home Secretary for submissions by interested parties. The Home Secretary has announced that a White or a Green Paper on the future of broadcasting will be published later in the year.

The Debate

The debate was far-ranging and covered virtually every aspect of the Annan Committee's report and recommendations. Inevitably, however, the major discussions centred around the recommendations on the fourth television channel and on local radio. The future of educational broadcasting too attracted many speakers.

Arising out of the reference back of paragraphs, or parts of paragraphs, of the NEC's report, a total of sixteen emergency propositions were submitted to the Standing Orders Committee. Of these, 12 were admitted to the agenda and carried, two were remitted to the NEC, one was ruled out of order and one was not adopted.

The heaviest burden of the day fell on the members of the Standing Orders Committee – Derek Cornell (chairman), Chris Atkinson, Eric Jacobs and Melvyn Silverman. (John Gray was unavoidably absent) – who had the task of co-ordinating propositions of similar intent from various branches into 'composites' acceptable to all concerned. In this they had the assistance of a member of the NEC.

John Elfes, Chairman of the Association

Allan Woods, Glasgow 1

Speakers

General Secretary Tony was the principal speaker for the platform; others included Senior Vice-Chairman Eric Stoves, Junior Vice-Chairman Grant Bremner, Derek Cutler, Reg Hutchings, Alan Bowler, BBC local radio representative Geoff Leonard, ILR representative Brian Lister, IBA representative Jim Walters and freelance representative Reggie Smith.

Taking a major part in the debate from the floor were Chris Jones (Brompton Road IBA) on the fourth television channel and educational broadcasting; Rodney Bennett, Ken Hoole, Doreen Taylor and Gordon Snell (Freelance) on a wide range of matters affecting freelance members; Mike Hollingworth (Radio Cleveland), Annette Maher (Radio Medway) and Heather Hampson (Piccadilly Radio) on the proposed Local Broadcasting Authority. Other speakers included Terry Sandland (St. Hilary), Denis Perry (Caversham 1), Chick Anthony (London TVS) and Allan Woods (Glasgow 1).

Observers included Nigel Fell of Radio Leeds (at present on attachment to Radio Leicester), Judith Weymont of Piccadilly Radio and Denis McShane, NEC member of the National Union of Journalists.

This was indeed a necessary special council in order to get the members' views on the detailed Annan report and seek their ratification of the National Executive's response to it.

Head Office Staff at Special Council

AGS (Admin.) Jack Rogers with the Head Office Staff who ensured the smooth running of Council. Left to right: Jack Rogers, Carol Walker, John Richards, Sue Radley and Gail Rodgers.

NEC members Geoff Leonard (BBC Local Radio) and Brian Lister (Independent Local Radio) listen attentively to Grant Bremner, the Association Junior Vice-Chairman.

BBC Staff Pay

Ever since I joined the BBC, pay was always an issue and it became more so once I started work at Television Centre. There were so many different pay grades it made it complicated and it took some considerable time to get one's head around it. We of course all understood that the public, in paying their licence fee, determined the amount of money the BBC had to spend.

BBC Television Members Pledge
Support in Fight on Pay

BBC members working in London Television gave their overwhelming support to the NEC's determination to fight for an adequate pay increase this year.

Two thousand members attending the mass meeting at the Odeon Hammersmith on Wednesday, 24 August virtually unanimously voted in favour of the NEC's proposition:

"This mass meeting of London Television members
1. supports the ABS's declared pay objectives;
2. supports the NEC's demand that the TUC must insist on a genuine return to free collective bargaining and oppose any attempt by government to interfere with the process of free collective bargaining in the public sector;
3. deplores the government's use of its power to determine the licence fee to bring improper and unacceptable pressure to bear on the BBC's freedom to negotiate with the recognised unions;
4. condemns the Government's policy on pay as set out in the White Paper, "The Attack on Inflation after July 1977;
5. rejects the arguments set out by the BBC's Chairman, Sir Michael Swann, in his message to staff dated 10 August 1977.

"The NEC, therefore, calls upon this meeting to pledge its full support for the united and disciplined action that will be necessary to achieve the Association's declared pay objectives."

The meeting also called on the NEC to set up a strike contingency fund to be administered by a strike committee.

The intensity of feeling about the erosion of real earnings, the pressure being brought to bear by the government and the total surrender of the management to this pressure was evident from the massive turnout on a day of torrential rain.

At the meeting, speaker after speaker expressed individual and branch willingness to take industrial action to secure a realistic settlement.

The members' anger was particularly directed against Sir Michael Swann's "message to staff" which was seen not only as "supine and abject surrender" to Government pressure but also totally unacceptable in the way in which it sought to deal with staff over the heads of the recognized unions.

General Secretary Tony Hearn, speaking on the NEC's proposition, told the meeting: "There is no resemblance between the Government's view of free collective bargaining and what the trade union movement wants."

"The Government," he said, "has shown that this (restriction) is not merely a desired policy but that it will use all the muscle — blackmail and force — at its command to enforce this policy."

Reminding the members of the need to beware of the BBC's tactics, Tony Hearn warned the members: "The fact is we have had a rough deal and there is no chance of the union successfully getting the settlement it wants if it is divided."

Senior Vice-Chairman Eric Stoves emphasised that: "The whole future of public service broadcasting, our job security, standards of living and our future depends on this, and we must win."

"It will be a war of attrition", he went on. "It is not going to be easy. It will be a couple of one-day strikes. It will be a case of weeks and maybe months."

No Offer

The National Joint Council (the BBC and the recognised unions) met on 25 August. The BBC formally tabled the Home Secretary's letter to the Chairman of the Board of Governors. It made no pay offer of any kind to the unions which asked that an offer be made as quickly as possible. The unions also supported the pay objectives set out by the ABS in a letter to the management sent in July.

Nevertheless, in comparison to other workers in commercial television and commercial radio our salaries were very low indeed. Hence, the demand from sections of staff to have their work re-appraised and upgraded. TV1 branch, with so many diverse pay scales within its membership, soon became used to submitting grading claims.

75

National Executive Resignations

Five members of the National Executive made their feelings very clear when they felt they had choice but to resign from the NEC due to it overriding a proposition on pay that had been overwhelmingly supported at Annual Conference. The proposition in question had been put forward by my own branch TV1 and had been fully supported by the Television IBLC. I was grateful that the other representatives from the IBLC backed me up. It was a matter of principal that, having put forward a proposition to Annual Council that was fully debated before being voted on and passed, I had no alternative but to resign when the NEC flouted that proposition.

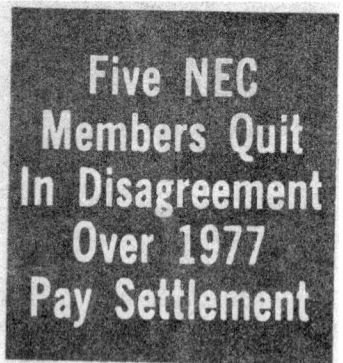

Five NEC Members Quit In Disagreement Over 1977 Pay Settlement

Disagreement over the decision taken in December last to discontinue industrial action and accept the BBC's offer on pay has led to the resignation of five members of the National Executive Committee.

The five, who sent their resignations to the ABS chairman John Elfes after the December NEC meeting, are:

Grant Bremner (TV 1), junior vice-chairman; Bill Jenkins (TV 5) and John Woolmer (TV 2) — all directly elected members; Barry Luckhurst (Acton 1), Technical Staff representative; and George Turner (TV 3), Weekly Staff representative.

Letter to the Editor:

> Sir, re the BBC pay offer and the ABS acceptance. May I ask are we a UNION or an old ladies' tea party? When the NEC react with such despicable cowardice (after only one shot across the bows) and fade away like clucking hens I have no doubt.
> Pass the biscuits please.
>
> **R. J. Pope**
> *London TV 1*

A letter condemning the NEC for its action

I should point out that four of us who had resigned were re-elected to the NEC at the Annual Council a few months later. I was junior vice-chairman of the Association at the time we resigned in December 1977 and was re-appointed to the same office after being re-elected at the Annual Council in April 1978.

Friends & Colleagues on the Executive Committee and Standing Orders Committee 1978:

Jenny Macarthur, Bill Jenkin and Brian Lister.

Left to right: Grant Bremner, Eric Jacobs, John Woolmer and John Elfes.

Pat Keogh and Charles Hutchison.

Standing Orders Committee, l. to r. Don Horne, Eric Jacobs, Asang, Melvyn Silverman, Chris Atkinson and John Gray.

This is the only decent photo I have of Melvyn Silverman

Industrial Disputes

The main reason there were so many industrial disputes with the BBC during the 70s and 80s was quite simply down to pay and conditions of service. BBC salaries across all grades were way behind our counterparts working for commercial television, such as Make-Up artists as mentioned earlier. All OP (Operational Grades) - cameramen, film and television, sound engineers, video tape and lighting engineers plus all the rest including production staff were grossly underpaid. A decade before, the BBC seemed to believe that you could afford to work for it, but times had changed. Therefore, union members wanted a decent salary and as the Television Inter-branch Liaison Committee had well over 8,000 members located not only at Television Centre but at all other BBC buildings in West London - Lime Grove, Ealing Film Studios, Kensington House, Costume Store plus many other smaller administration buildings, there were many disputes involving industrial action by various sections of the union membership right across the board. Production Assistants had a fairly lengthy dispute that lasted 7 weeks, but eventually they returned to work feeling let down by Tony Hearn the General Secretary.

Strikes:

There were numerous authorised strikes during the 70s and the 80s and there is no doubt whatsoever that industrial relations with the BBC was at an all-time low. Union members and of course all staff took pride in their work but there was a genuine feeling that the BBC did not fully appreciate their talents. Individual grading claims, of which there were over two hundred separate claims at one point, were not the real answer to pay being so low throughout the BBC. So it was inevitable that when negotiations failed, the only recourse for the union was to take industrial action in support of their justified pay claim or changes in their conditions of service.

Industrial action was not taken lightly, members were always consulted to find their strength of feeling, and whether they were committed to possible industrial action. Back then union members who took industrial action were deducted pay for doing so, the same as applies today, therefore, industrial action through striking was always our last resort.

Mass Meetings:

Towards the latter part of the 70s mass meetings of ABS members were becoming commonplace due to low pay and poor conditions of service imposed by the BBC. A mass meeting of Television Centre members at the Hammersmith Odeon with me in the chair was held on 24th August 1977. This was followed by another mass meeting of central London members at the RIBA Theatre on 13th September.

Mass Meeting at Hammersmith Odeon:

Two thousand members working in London Television gave their overwhelming support to the NEC's determination to fight for an adequate pay increase this year. The intensity of feelings about the erosion of real earnings being brought to bear by the government and the total surrender of the BBC management to this pressure was evident from the massive turnout on a day of torrential rain.

At Hammersmith
L. to r. Maisie Wiley, Terry Cornelius, John Woolmer, Barry Luckhurst, Eric Stoves, Chairman Grant Bremner, G S Tony Hearn, DGS Paddy Leech, Jean Harvey, Geoff Leonard, Celia Croasdell, Jack Rogers.

At the meeting, speaker after speaker expressed individual and branch willingness to take industrial action to secure a realistic settlement. The members' anger was particularly directed against Sir Michael Swann's 'message to staff,' which was seen not only as 'supine and abject surrender' to Government pressure, but also totally unacceptable in the way in which it sought to deal with staff over the heads of the recognised unions. The senior vice-chairman emphasised that: 'The whole future of public service broadcasting, our job security, standards of living and our future depends on this, and we must win.'

Mass Meeting at RIBA Central London:

In Central London
L. to r. Jean Harvey, DGS Paddy Leech, GS Tony Hearn, Chairman John Elfes, Eric Stoves, Grant Bremner and Maisie Wiley

Seven hundred and fifty ABS members working for the BBC in Central London swung solidly behind the NEC in its call for disciplined industrial action to force a realistic 1977 pay settlement and went on to vote overwhelmingly for an organised campaign to preserve the standards of public service broadcasting.

Other Branch Disputes

In early January 1978 the BBC took the decision to suspend staff and send them home if they took authorised strike actions and TV2 were the union members affected.

Suspensions Weapon: BBC Management Defied
London TV2 Members Back To Work

Background:

The immediate background that led to industrial action and the suspension of TV2 members began at the end of November 1977 when the procedure agreement had been exhausted following failure to resolve the hours of work dispute at ACAS. From the beginning of December, TV2 members, with NEC sanction, refused to work in Studio TC1 and to carry out work on programmes after midnight. While the BBC rescheduled its programmes to end at 11.45pm, negotiations resumed at national level between the General Secretary and BBC Controller, Staff Administration. The ABS did not react to the BBC's decision to maintain late transmissions over the holiday period by use of managerial labour.

Suspensions:

On Friday 6th January 1978, while negotiations were still in progress, the management started to suspend without pay TV2 members carrying out official instructions of the NEC. As chairman of the TV Sub-Divisional Committee, I was informed of this just minutes before Dick Craig took this action. He had telephoned me to tell me he was about to suspend two TV News members and I rushed there in time to see it happen and to give them my support. By Sunday night January 8th, 21 members had been suspended. Other suspensions in large numbers were to follow. Television programmes on Saturday January 7th were disrupted when the duty shift withdrew its labour on the instruction of the NEC.

Blank Screens:

It was on Saturday evening I drove into Television Centre around 6pm and went to our union office, and as Chairman of the TV SDC (Sub-divisional committee) I had arranged for other key union representatives to meet me there. The strike notices had been printed the previous day by our secretary Vivian Bellman. Off we went at around 6.45pm into the video tape suites where Bruce Forsythe's Generation Game, which had been recorded on the Friday, was being broadcast. The programme was at the stage when the winner was about to choose their prizes from the moving belt when the Video Tape engineer, a union member, after reading the strike notice immediately stopped the video tape from playing, reversed the tape then made the machine safe before he walked out of the suite. Of course television screens went blank across the whole of the United Kingdom. Back in the office we sat and watched the blank screen on the small portable TV we'd purchased, delighted with our success.

Blank Screen

We had taken management by complete surprise, and it was almost two hours later before Dick Craig arrived with a few other managers and programmes were eventually restored.

TV2 Emergency Meeting:

Over 200 TV2 members attended an emergency meeting at the Bush Hotel, Shepherds Bush on Monday 9th January. Reports were received from Tony Hearn and ABS chairman John Elfes and TV2 committee members and me. Overwhelming support was given for the need to continue industrial action both to force a reasonable settlement and to protect suspended colleagues. The walkout by the scheduled TV2 shift on the Monday further escalated the dispute when the management suspended the entire shift, bringing the total number of suspensions on the evening of Wednesday, 11th January to 162 ABS members.

Consultation at the London TV2 Committee meeting. Left to right: John Armstrong, John Woolmer, General Secretary Tony Hearn and ABS Chairman John Elfes.

Other Branches:

By now members of TV5 and Television News branches had also been suspended for refusal to co-operate with blacked programmes being operated by managerial or non-union labour. As a result of the further suspensions the NEC on Thursday, 12th January instructed all TV2 and all Television News members to withdraw their labour.
It further instructed all members working in London Television to attend a mass meeting at the Hammersmith Odeon on the following day at noon.

Mass Meeting:

Over 1,600 members packed the Odeon on 13th January 1978 for a two-hour heated debate. The following motion was carried overwhelmingly: "This mass meeting of members of the ABS working in London Television (1) condemns the use by the BBC of the legal weapon of alleged breach of contract by individual members as a method of solving complex industrial problems; (2) pledges its full support for any steps that the NEC takes to protect those members suspended without pay for alleged breach of contract and to settle on agreed terms the substantive issues in dispute between the ABS (on behalf of its TV2 members) and the BBC".

Television members arrive at the Odeon

No to Total Strike: A proposal from the TV IBLC, calling for a total strike by all ABS members if a solution could not be reached within seven days was narrowly defeated by a show of hands.

Conclusion:

Talks lasting until late on Friday, January 13th brought a dramatic end to the dispute which had resulted in over 500 ABS members being suspended or on strike. In meetings which lasted from early afternoon until 10.00pm, the General Secretary, the deputy general secretary and the chairman of the Association bargained with newly appointed BBC Director of Personnel, Michael Bett and other senior management representatives to find a formula to end the dispute. All suspended members were reinstated and an agreement was reached that hours would not be scheduled after midnight.

Other news for January 1978

That good news was followed later in the month by bad news when the favourite pub of the ABS was **virtually** demolished in a gas explosion.

Blast Rocks "ABS Pub"

A huge explosion virtually demolished the Valiant Trooper, the pub next door to the ABS office about mid-day Wednesday, Jan 25. Early reports indicated that the cause was a gas explosion. Apparently road workers, digging up nearby Goodge Street had drilled through a gas main. Press reports said that a total of twenty-five people were injured, some of whom had to be taken to hospital. The explosion occurred about 12.30 pm when the pub was already filling up but not, as it would have been half an hour later, packed. The Valiant Trooper was frequently used by ABS Head Office staff and by ABS members at Head Office after meetings. Nobody connected with the Association was in the pub at the time. ABS windows along Whitfield Street were smashed by the force of the explosion and three members of staff (Brian Marsh, Alan Jones and Sue Radley) were showered with glass. As a precaution, the office was closed and the staff were sent home for the rest of the afternoon.

Valiant Trooper Severely Damaged

Tony Hearn Gets a New Secretary/PA

MEET YOUR HEAD OFFICE STAFF

Sue Radley was, until recently, secretary to AGS Doug Smith. However, she is now moving into the hot-seat vacated by Asang as secretary to Tony Hearn. Asang has left the Association to go and live in India. The best of luck, Sue!

Having joined the ABS in 1973, working first for Nick Bunyan and then for Doug Smith, in September 1978 Sue accepted promotion to work for Tony following the departure of Asang (formerly Margaret) to go and live in India to meditate and follow her dream.

Further Disputes and Strikes

Leading up to Christmas 1978 another pay dispute led to a series of actions that were to cause programmes to not be transmitted. As the dispute continued, and against Tony Hearn's advice, I negotiated with Roger Chase as to what programmes would show a blank screen with the caption, 'This programme is not being broadcast due to industrial action by the Association of Broadcasting & Allied Staffs.' It was his opinion that the public would blame the union for the loss of the programme. I held the opposite view that we wanted the public to know we were taking action against the BBC. Every morning we would meet in Roger Chase's office and go through the programme schedule for the day and decide which programmes would not be transmitted and would be replaced with the agreed notice.

The agreed statement on the television when programmes were off the air

The dispute went on for over two weeks until there was a meeting arranged at ACAS, but we continued to take programmes off air during that time, right up until the dispute was settled.

Picket Line Television Centre:

21–22 December 1978 – BBC1 and BBC2 are forced off the air due to industrial action at the BBC by the ABS union which starts on Thursday 21 December. The following day the radio unions join their BBC Television counterparts, forcing the BBC to merge their four national radio networks into one national radio station, the BBC All Network Radio Service, from 4pm that afternoon. The strike is settled shortly before 10pm on 22 December with the unions and BBC management reaching an agreement at the British government's industrial disputes arbitration service ACAS. BBC1 resumes broadcast at 3pm on Saturday 23 December with BBC2 resuming at 1pm the same afternoon. Threat of disruption to the BBC's festive television schedules is averted. BBC Radio networks resume normal schedules on the morning of Saturday 23 December.

There was a large picket line outside the main entrance to Television Centre and being December it was freezing cold, so Ernie Johnston a union officer asked the BBC if we could have a brazier on their premises by the gate. They agreed which made it much better and warmer for the picket line. The BBC had just paid the outrageous sum of seven million pounds for the rights to broadcast the film The Sound of Music, so we had banners made asking those in passing cars to 'toot if you hate the sound of music' and every toot was music to our ears. A large meeting was held at the Hammersmith Apollo Theatre, attended by union members from all over the Television Directorates.

It was a lengthy strike and we finally ended at ACAS, an organisation that arbitrates between employer and workers when they are in dispute and ask for their services. I had been there often enough in the past, so they knew me quite well. The talks were lengthy and spanned two whole days finally finishing at 8pm on a Friday night with what was called the 'Schedule 11 award'. In essence it gave all BBC staff a 16% pay increase. The word had reached Television Centre that an agreement had been reached at ACAS and the management asked the pickets to disperse. Ernie Johnston apparently told them, 'Not until I hear it from Grant Bremner.' It was half an hour later before I arrived exhausted at Television Centre and informed them it was over. We all then adjourned to the BBC club on the fourth floor and had a well-deserved drink. We were joined by Dick Craig who was genuinely pleased with our achievement.

TV1 Members Strike:

Vice-chairman Grant Bremner and pickets outside TVC main gate on Aug 15.

Producers' Assistant members of TV1 branch took industrial action on 15th August 1979.

TV 5 Strike:

Another industrial action I want to mention also occurred in 1979. That strike was by members of TV5 branch: cameramen, lighting, sound etc., all on OP grades, which turned out to be different than the rest. This was not just about pay, but conditions of service, working hours etc. Talks with management had got nowhere so the branch Chairman John Barlow conducted a pole amongst his members and ascertained there were enough members willing to strike. Tony Hearn was against such action but the branch prevailed and the TV5 strike began. It was to last three weeks before a settlement was reached but it was remarkable for a number of reasons: the resolve of the branch members to hold out although they were not being paid and the support given to TV5 by other branches within Television. John Barlow and Bill Jenkin put forward the suggestion that it would be helpful if the union could support the members by paying some money, this was rejected by the National Executive Committee on the advice of Tony Hearn.

The Television IBLC then decided to try and raise money to help TV5 members by holding information meetings right across all Television buildings where donations to the strike fund were sought.

I can't remember the precise number of meetings that were held, but there were many where representatives of TV5 branch put forward their detailed grievances, hence the reason for the strike. A large meeting was held at the Hammersmith Apollo where Tony Hearn asked me to chair the meeting.

Another large meeting was held in a cinema near Hammersmith Broadway and I noticed Vanessa Redgrave, the actress, drop £20 into a bucket, very big-hearted indeed. Those who attended the meeting were very generous as well, over twenty thousand in cash was collected, and it was necessary to open a bank account in Shepherds Bush in which to deposit the money. The strike was eventually settled although not all members of TV5 were completely satisfied with the result. The money that had been collected was divided up by TV5 branch representatives and given to those members who had taken strike action.

There were of course many more industrial disputes involving different sections of BBC staff, Television Production Assistants, Video Tape Editors across the whole BBC not just at Television Centre. Roger Chase asked me if I would facilitate a meeting between the management and the regional union representative Derek Cutler and when contacted he said yes. Roger Chase drove me down to the meeting along the M4 to a pub/restaurant on the outskirts of Bristol where we were joined by Derek and Dick Craig. We enjoyed a meal first then adjourned to a private room where we discussed the current impasse. No agreement was made, we were still too far apart. Roger dove me home cautiously and slowly, having imbibed rather too much, and I arrived home at 2am on the Saturday morning.

Local Radio Under Threat

The second report of the Home Office local radio working party was published on 23rd July 1979 and the

ABS's views were given in a letter from the general secretary to the secretary of the working party on 6th August in which he stated "I was horrified when I read the second report of the Home Office local radio working party. It has confirmed the worst fears that my union had when the working party was set up".

Letter to home secretary

On the same day, Aug 6, the general secretary wrote to the Home Secretary the Rt Hon William Whitelaw enclosing a copy of the letter to the secretary of the local radio working party and a copy of the article on the fourth channel that appeared in the August ABStract. The general secretary said that taken together the letter and the article reflected the grave concern of the ABS at current developments affecting the future of British broadcasting. "We believe" he said "that there is now a very real danger that in both television and radio the present balance between the BBC and the IBA will be destroyed and that the main driving force in British broadcasting will no longer be public service but commercial profit. I cannot believe that this is what the government intends to happen." The general secretary asked for an urgent meeting with the Home Secretary.

(An ABS team including general secretary Tony Hearn, chairman Eric Stoves and vice-chairman Grant Bremner are due to meet the home secretary on Wednesday, 12th September.)

The meeting with William Whitelaw, the Home Secretary, took place at the Home Office and the General Secretary pressed home the ABS's strongly held opinion regarding the future of BBC local radio and our opposition and severe reservations about a number of paragraphs contained within the Local Radio working party's report especially as we had not been invited to participate.

Overseas Union Business

Over the years I went on three overseas trips for the ABS, the first being a trip to the USA to New York & Washington DC, the second to Paris and the third to Rome.

New York & Washington DC:

Co-productions with other broadcasting organisations were getting off the ground in the UK, Europe, and the United States of America and of course this caused a number of issues, such as who would be allowed to work cameras, sound equipment and associated staff. I had been elected as the chairman of the co-production committee to look into this.

Initially I held a meeting with Gary Richmond, assistant to Roger Chase, who had been tasked with looking into co-productions from a BBC point of view. Gary was of the opinion that we should travel together to the USA to discuss the subject with USA broadcasting outlets and various unions. I was in total agreement with this joint venture, however when I put this to Tony Hearn he was utterly opposed to the BBC paying for me. So, I went to New York on my own for a week and Jack Rogers the administration officer booked me into what I can only call a very shabby hotel on 7th Avenue where I only stayed for one night, after which I booked myself into the Chelsea Hotel the following morning. I held several meetings with various broadcasting unions in New York who were very hospitable and they even asked after our General Secretary Tony Hearn. One day I came across an ENG unit (Electronic News Gathering) waiting outside a subway station that was closed off with police tape. They told me they were waiting for a body to be brought up, the victim of a shooting, a not uncommon occurrence apparently. Welcome to the USA! My visit to Washington to meet representatives from ABC was only a day trip when I took a return flight down to Washington.

However, I do believe the union missed out on valuable contacts, as Gary also travelled to San Francisco and Los Angeles (and I bet he stayed in much better hotels), although I did manage to celebrate my birthday while in New York by treating myself to half a Maine Lobster in a nice restaurant.

> **Co-productions**
>
> The Television sub-divisional committee has over the past few years discussed co-productions with the television directorate, the attitude taken of late by the co-production committee has been more flexible taking into account the financial position of the BBC and I am confident that this attitude will prevail. However, I certainly would like more details as to how "co-productions will emerge in new forms and between new parties"?
>
> Mr Checkland refers to new technology and throwing in a Chyron or two, may I remind him that the future of electronic graphics has been of concern to the ABS for the past couple of years and we have been patiently waiting for the BBC's detailed proposals for this particular field. To this date we have had none. Reference is made to the purchase and development of videotape machines on different formats and also the development by some bright spark of digital VT. I would question at this stage a decision by the television directorate to have allowed a situation where currently there are three separate formats within VT that will expand well into the latter end of the eighties and remind the management that during the evaluation of the VPR1s the ABS pointed out to management that in their belief digital VT machines would probably be available within the next four or five years and should we not then consider the question of one or two formats for videotape — never mind three or four. Mr Checkland states "off we go again". I do not doubt that within the middle of the eighties he will be correct and off we will go again on the evaluation of another format for VT machines whilst we are still equipping with VPR2s or its equivalent. The question is posed in relation to manning arrangements, in particular "have we kept in line with changing production methods?". The answer I would give is an emphatic no. We have not kept in line with changing production methods in relation to rehearse / record techniques but has the BBC approached the unions over the past two or three years about rehearse / record and new production techniques in relation to manning levels?
>
> W. Grant Bremner
> *Chairman, Television SDC*

Grant Bremner, chairman Television SDC

• • •

Later, back in the UK, I was in a good position to write about co-productions in the union magazine, ABStract, in response to an article written by Mike Checkland.

As it later turned out within the television and film industry, co-productions became joint enterprises with some putting up the finance, while others the equipment and the workforce. Today co-productions are very commonplace within the broadcasting and film media.

Paris:

Tony Hearn, Eric Stoves and my good self travelled to Paris to meet up with the French Broadcasting Unions. Tony was accompanied by his wife and his Secretary, Sue Radley, also accompanied us. Alan Sapper, General Secretary of the ACCT union, was also present. It was an intensive time as the French, being the French, included a very long working lunch that lasted several hours. There were several interesting things that occurred during that trip. Tony evidently hoped that Sue would keep his wife, Anne, company while we went off to meet the French union representatives, which she duly did for the morning, but took the opportunity to go exploring on her own in the afternoon while Anne had a rest. Later on in the evening when in a French restaurant, Anne heard the waiter explain to me the fish I was interested in. She decided to order the same, but when it came she complained loudly that the fish should be flat but was not. Although it was actually sole, it was stuffed with a sauce with prawns in the middle, as had been explained! On another occasion she asked for a well-done steak, not what a French Chef would appreciate. She asked Sue who was the only person present who could speak French to send it back three times, until Tony got upset and said she'd be better off in the USA where she could have burnt steak to her heart's content.

Rome:

On this occasion we were going to a three-day conference organised by the Italian Broadcasting Unions and Tony Hearn took the decision that we should travel out on a Friday so we would have a couple of days free over the weekend to visit the sights, which was generous of him. There were five of us on this occasion, Tony Hearn, Eric Stoves, Alan Bowler, myself and Sue Radley.

We duly arrived at Rome Airport around eight o'clock in the evening and Tony, instead of waiting for the car that was to pick us up and take us to our hotel, accepted the first taxi that approached. Needless to say we took the longest route to the hotel passing the same places twice and when we eventually arrived at our hotel the driver demanded a king's ransom. Luckily one of the Italian union representatives overheard the heated conversation and came to our rescue. We have no idea what he told the illegal taxi driver but he got back into his taxi and shot away, I don't think any money changed hands.

The following day Sue and I went to see the Roman Baths and lo and behold we came across Sue Pringle, one of Tony's previous secretaries who was in Rome studying Italian - the world is certainly a small place. However, the conference due to start on the Monday was postponed until the following day, so we only attended two days as Jack Rogers, our Administration Officer had booked our flights back to the UK on the Thursday.

Hotel Parco Dei Principe Rome: I have to say that the Italian unions did us proud indeed, although we later learnt that it was the Italian government that was paying for the conference, the accommodation plus meals and drinks. The five-star Parco Dei Principe is to this day the best hotel I have ever stayed in. The approach was impressive with the two lions guarding the entrance, the rooms were lavishly furnished and oozed comfort which was duplicated throughout the hotel. The dining room was something to behold with white linen cloths on the tables and waiters in white aprons waiting to serve you.

At dinner we met John Wilson, the General Secretary of NATTKE (National Association of Theatrical, Television and Kine Employees) who informed Sue and I that we could choose from the 'A La Carte' menu and not the printed one on the table, which of course we did each evening. The meals were simply superb and thoroughly enjoyable. It was in this hotel that I tasted the best ever Parmigiano (Parmesan) cheese, it just melted in the mouth. I remember we tipped the maid on leaving and she thrust soap and an ashtray into our hands as she appeared so grateful for the tip. I'm quite sure that if I was to try and book a room here for just one night I would not be able to afford it.

Annual Conference

The union held annual general meetings to discuss and vote upon motions put forward by the various branches for debate, to elect members of the National Executive

Committee, and to agree the union finances. The NEC had previously discussed these motions and either supported or opposed them and had selected speakers from the executive to speak at conference.

My first conference was in 1974 and my last in 1986 (although I did miss the one held in Guernsey in 1985 having recently been appointed as Dresser Manager in Costume Department). I became very accustomed to public speaking and debate and I was not afraid to approach the microphone and say my piece either in support of a motion or against it. I felt confident in my words and performance. On one occasion, as a branch representative in support of my own motion that was opposed by the national executive, I was putting forward the case that a percentage pay rise only benefitted those on the higher pay bands, and the majority of my members in TV1 branch, and any other branch with low paid members, would benefit from a flat sum pay increase instead. I was supported by a number of other branches and the motion was won by a handsome majority, much to the dismay of the General Secretary who of course would now have to negotiate this with the BBC. We did in fact that year receive a flat sum payment which did indeed benefit those in lower pay bands.

My last Conference was in 1986 when I attended as a delegate representing the Managerial branch, London TV7. By now, despite my 3 month stay in hospital the previous summer/autumn, I had settled into my role as Dresser Manager in Costume Department.

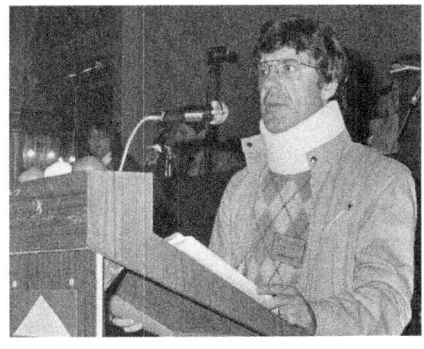

Historically the meetings had taken place in May and were held in large conference hotels in Blackpool, Hastings or Brighton. However, in 1975 the date was moved to April to enable the use of cheaper university premises, a policy followed for the next 5 years at both Reading and Guildford, staying in the student accommodation, where the administration officer obviously got a very good deal.

Industrial Relations Officers BBC

The BBC employed two Industrial Relations Officers, Hans Norton and Leslie Price who usually attended meetings when grading issues were being discussed and were at most negotiating meetings. I found it especially interesting that the year TV1 branch had put forward the motion asking the executive to negotiate a flat sum pay award and not a percentage increase, Hans Norton was given an invitation to attend the annual conference by the General Secretary. I spoke to the motion on behalf of my branch saying, 'one percent of sod all is sod all, yet £500 is fair to all.' The motion was overwhelmingly carried even though the executive committee spoke against it.

The following week after conference I received in confidence from a good union friend a copy of a long and detailed statement by Hans Norton to the Controller BBC and Senior Management quoting almost every word I had said in defence of my motion. 'Bremner got them so worked up the executive was bound to lose.' Now I was very annoyed that Hans Norton had been invited to our conference and clearly he was secretly there as a spy. So, I went to see Tony Hearn and told him I was annoyed at the actions of this man spying and reporting back on me to his bosses. Tony after reading the document was annoyed about the comment 'the executive was bound to lose.' He immediately contacted the then Director of Personnel at Broadcasting House to make a formal complaint. All hell then broke loose at Broadcasting House as the BBC made stringent efforts to try and trace the individual who had sent me the statement. They never did, I am delighted to say.

Accused of Attempted Murder

This was a very strange accusation made against me at an executive committee meeting, a totally outrageous and frankly unbelievable comment made by Tony Hearn the General Secretary.

These are the events that led up to the accusation. One day I was due to have a grading meeting with management and union members from the Duty Office. The union officer who would accompany me to the meeting was

Doug Smith. He arrived at Television Centre in time for the meeting around 12.30 and I asked him where the file on this grading case was. He replied he'd left it back in the office at Goodge Street. I said I can't hold the meeting without it and asked could he go back and get it or get someone to bring it to Television Centre, and I would get the meeting put back an hour or so. He agreed to go back to the office and collect it. He never retuned and when I telephoned the office in Goodge Street I was informed that when he arrived back at the Goodge Street office, he apparently collapsed and after getting two stiff brandies from Jack Rogers, our admin officer, he went home saying he had a heart problem.

Time passed and a couple of months later during an executive meeting when I was on my feet speaking Tony Hearn for some unknown reason, other than he probably did not like what I was saying, said in very loud and exaggerated voice clearly in anger, 'Bremner you very nearly murdered one of my officers, I won't have anything to do with you,' and he then stormed out of the meeting. I was completely taken aback and of course I assumed he must have been talking about Doug Smith who had still not returned to work. I demanded an apology and asked the then President Eric Stoves to insist that he return to the executive meeting and apologise to me. Eric reluctantly went to find Tony and after several minutes he came back saying that Tony's union representative had informed him the General Secretary had gone home feeling unwell. A few days later when Tony returned to the office he rang the Director of Personnel Television, Roger Chase, and told him not to deal with me, Grant Bremner, on any union matter.

Roger Chase informed him that as I was the elected Chairman of the Television Inter-Branch Liaison Committee he would continue to deal with me as before and that he did not take instruction from him. Tony then clearly had words with some of his officers who cold-shouldered me at executive meetings as if I had indeed attempted to murder an officer. The officer concerned stayed off work for six months and only came back to work with some alacrity when Tony threatened to stop his pay until his return to duties.

Finally the executive committee led by a very good friend insisted that the General Secretary write to me and apologise to me for calling me a murderer. It was ironic that he had to dictate the letter to Sue Radley who was now his secretary.

Chairmanship / Presidency of the Union

Prior to a rule change at Conference in 1980, the Chairman, Senior Vice Chairman and Junior Vice Chairman were appointed from within the NEC at its first meeting after Conference. The normal practice was to serve as junior vice chairman for 2 years, moving up to two years as senior vice chairman and then serving as chairman for two years. I served as junior vice-chairman in 1977 and 1978, then became senior vice-chairman in 1979. However, at Conference 1980 rule changes were agreed providing for the positions to be re-titled to President and two Vice-Presidents to be elected from the whole membership of the Association by ballot at Annual Conference (effective from 1981). Following Conference 1980 at the first meeting of the NEC when a chairman and two vice-chairman were appointed for the last time before the new rules, Eric Stoves was appointed for a third year as Chairman, and indeed was elected to serve as the first President the following year at the Annual conference in Brighton in 1981. At that conference in 1981 I was elected as Vice-President along with Alan Bowler.

Eric Stoves (President), Alan Bowler (Vice President), Grant Bremner (Vice President)

The following year at Conference in 1982, Alan Bowler was elected as President with myself and Eric Stoves as Vice-Presidents. At this point it became clear to me that I would never be elected as President given the power base I had back at Television Centre and associated buildings. In truth I was rather pleased as I was beginning to feel it was time to advance my career within the BBC as I had been AIC of the Television Gramophone Library for several years now, and although I had managed to get the post regraded to a management grade on MP1, I wanted a new challenge. However, it was to be another three years before that opportunity came.

The Authority of the Word BLACKED

I first came across this term in the BBC when a union member at Ealing Film Studios called to inform me that he had informed the management that he had 'blacked' a piece of film that had come from an outside source due to its inferior quality and would I support him. He went on to explain that the piece of film in contention should have been shot by his members and he believed cheaper labour had been used as the film had been taken at night and the Ealing Film management did not want to pay overtime. I drove to Ealing and was shown the piece of film in question, which was clearly of an inferior quality, so without hesitation along with John we went to see the manager and informed him the film had been 'blacked' and no union member would touch it. To my surprise this statement was accepted by the management without too much argument.

That single incident was to be the catalyst of many other incidents of 'blacked' film, video tape and new equipment the BBC was trying to force upon our members without conducting any negotiations.

The Riley Graphics Dispute

In 1982 I received a telephone call from a nervous Bernard Simpson, a manager in the Graphics Department at Lime Grove, asking if he could meet with me to discuss a problem, a request I readily agreed to. I said I would come to their place of work at Lime Grove to see what the problem was. He brought with him to the meeting his deputy Brian, and they told me about a new graphics machine called Riley that was capable of putting graphic text directly onto a screen for transmission.

They then showed the kind of work that they did and it was clear to me that there was a big problem here, and that their department was in serious trouble if there was no intervention by the union. I asked how many of the staff were members of the union, none were. I said that in order for me to take this case up with the management there would have to be some members of the union in the department. I told Bernard that I would hold a recruitment meeting at 7pm in Threshold House and have an officer from head office present if he would bring his staff along. I telephoned Sue and she got hold of Nick Bunyan who rather reluctantly agreed to come along. Surprisingly all staff members turned up and I went through what I thought the union could do to help using the much-used phrase, 'unity in strength and strength in unity.' At the conclusion of the meeting they all signed the union membership forms I had asked Nick to bring along. I also remember that Nick borrowed £5 from me which I never saw again!

Character Generator in Situ

The following week on the Friday I was informed that Martin Hopkins, a well known Sports Producer at Lime Grove, was going to schedule a secretary to use the Riley machine on Grandstand the following afternoon. I immediately telephoned Dick Craig, Head of Personnel Television Engineering, and told him that the Riley machine was now 'blacked' and that nobody had better touch it until this matter was resolved or further action would be taken. Dick Craig then informed the production that they could not use the machine which of course did not please Martin Hopkins. I held another meeting with the new members of my own branch TV1 and informed them of the situation. I went on to say in confidence that I believed the best way to proceed with this was for me to ask the management to train all of the staff concerned on how to use a typewriter followed by training on the Riley machine itself, a tall order indeed. Only one or two of the new members had a basic idea of typing.

Martin Hopkins demanded a meeting with me to discuss the 'unblacking' of the Riley machine to which I agreed as I wanted him to know the strength of feeling the ABS had regarding this issue. The meeting took place at Television Centre in the basement near the video tape area, it was of my choosing as I wanted him away from his power base at Lime Grove. I was very surprised to see Bernard Simpson there as part of the management team, and I decided I would make sure he did not speak on their behalf, he'd been put in a difficult situation.

Martin opened by saying that secretaries were very capable of using this piece of equipment, so what was my problem. I told him that by doing so they would be putting my members out of a job and that was something I would not allow. I also explained the machine in question was much more than an electronic typewriter. He got annoyed and said the graphics staff could not even type. I went on to say that there was a simple remedy and that the BBC could train them. This appeared to annoy him further so he then said, 'I know for a fact one of them is dyslexic, maybe they all are.' Dick Craig rolled his eyes as knew without a doubt what was coming. I stood up and spoke, 'You are lucky I don't black the whole Grandstand Programme for that insult to my members, the equipment is blacked across the whole BBC,' and I left the room.

Further meetings took place with the management with Dick Craig and Duncan Thomas present and it was clear to me that Dick was sympathetic to my demand that the staff of the graphics department responsible for the making up and printing of on-screen graphics were to be retained instead of losing their jobs. Although Duncan Thomas was opposed to this idea he couldn't articulate his reasons clearly. Ultimately my view prevailed and an agreement was drawn up to the effect that the staff in the graphics section would be given typing lessons and within a month their training started.

There is no doubt that this was a major success for TV1 branch, firstly in being able to recruit the members from graphics department in order to show to the management the strength of feeling and secondly, our ability to 'black' a piece of electronic equipment and stop others from using it even though they had been instructed to do so by management. This was the first time the use of the word 'black' would be used in Television Centre to secure a victory over BBC management.

At my retirement leaving party in January 1989 the Riley Team - from left to right they are: Brian - Alastair Bremner (my son) - Me - Bernard Simpson - Roy Davis (Chairman TV1) - Keith

This is a note in my retirement book that reads as follows.

Well mate this is it - for many years I have printed the standard plate in the Print Room i.e. from your many colleagues & friends etc. in gold, not for you bruv! It's a personal thank you from me & the gang for all your hard work & support over the years - without you the Graphic Design Print Room would not exist. Kindest Regards Mate & all the Very Best.
Bernard Simpson – Keith Johnson

TUC Conferences

As an office holding member of the NEC I attended a few TUC Conferences over the years. They were mostly held in Blackpool and lasted a week.

ABStract October/November 1981

TUC Delegation

Tony Hearn, General Secretary, Alan Bowler, President

Eric Stoves, Vice-President, Grant Bremner, Vice-President

On this particular occasion congress moved to the left, decisively with little effective opposition, on economic policy, unilateral disarmament, and withdrawal from the EEC – the main issues on the order paper of congress. On the Tuesday afternoon Michael Foot made what was considered by many of those who heard it as his best public speech for a long time. He referred, amongst other things, to the internal problems of the Labour Party – an issue although not on the agenda of congress dominated the week as delegates were subjected to the attentions of the contenders for the deputy leadership of the party (and their ubiquitous hangers on).

Breakfast TV Negotiations

Late in the summer of 1982 the BBC announced that it wanted to start Breakfast TV so it could compete with commercial TV's AM programme. This announcement had a number of implications for staff and the union. All Production staff would be required to come in in the middle of the night, around 3am, to ensure that the live programme went out at 6.40am. This included cameramen, sound and lighting engineers, vision mixers, graphics staff, production assistants, scene hands and even secretaries. There was also new graphics equipment that had to be taken into account and of course conditions of service and hours of work. BBC management tried to present all of this grouped together, but the newly named Television SDC (Sub-Divisional Committee) of which I was still chairman, was opposed to this suggestion. We wanted to have negotiations on each affected group as there were so many different grades involved. In the end we landed up at ACAS and for reasons I still can't comprehend today, Tony Hearn only appeared once and told me, 'You can handle it Grant,' before he left.

It was rather surreal to be sat opposite a row of management, six or seven of them with an occasional department manager brought into the room with me leading the negotiations with union representatives representing different categories of staff that came and went throughout the following four days. Agreements were eventually made and a document detailing all of them was submitted to the National Executive Committee for approval.

You may remember that a live programme starting at 06.30am requires many staff to be on duty at 3.00am. It was clear that the BBC desperately wanted breakfast Television to proceed at all costs, being way behind commercial TV in this regard, and of course this played into our hands perfectly. Night payments enhanced, irregular hour payments and a number of upgrades within the graphics department and number of other improvements specific to Breakfast TV were finally agreed.

Front Page of BBC Staff Magazine January 1982

Many union members benefitted from the agreements struck over Breakfast Television, but it did change their lives with having to come into work so early.

Odd Thing to do for the Union Magazine

Alan Jones was the editor of the ABS magazine ABStract and, probably because he did not have enough copy, he asked if I would write a review of new LP recordings that came out monthly as I guess with my background in music he considered me to be an expert in that field. This I was pleased to do, but under the name of **S Grant**. I wrote this column for a couple of years before the executive decided to stop it as it was not union content in their eyes, a view with which I totally agreed. It had provided light and interesting reading nonetheless.

I thought it odd when, a couple of years later, miscellaneous book reviews appeared.

ABS Banner

Members of the NEC proudly displaying the new ABS banner in 1981. The banner was used on many occasions during marches in support of many good causes.

Ups and Downs

It has to be said that throughout my union days there were of course high points and conversely some low points, not everything came out smelling of roses. However, here's one that did. Graphic Design had sent out two of the Riley Operators on an Outside Broadcast and there happened to be industrial action back at

Television Centre where I had issued strike notices to other Riley operators who were working in the studio. Duncan Thomas sent a personnel officer Ian ? (sorry my memory has let me down even though he was a friend) to the outside broadcast and he told them they were sacked for obeying a union instruction and told them to go home. I only got to hear about this when one of them called me on his way to catch the train. I instructed him to go back to work and to get the personnel officer to call me urgently if he was still there, he wasn't he'd gone back to Television Centre.

The following week we discovered that the two Riley Operators in question had been deducted pay for not being at work, which of course they had been. I called the personnel officer concerned and informed him that neither I nor any member of my branch committee would deal with him as a representative of Graphic Design Department until their pay had been restored and they had received an apology. The matter was resolved the next day, a definite up.

Personal cases came along quite frequently, with thousands of union members this was bound to occur. There was one such case, a woman who was often late arriving for work.

The first time this happened, in her defence I said I myself had used the 220 bus from Wimbledon to Television Centre and it was often late, this was accepted, but she was warned about arriving late. On the second occasion I said she would buy an alarm clock and get up a bit earlier as the buses were still bad on that particular route. Steve Ansell smiled at me, then said, 'Hasn't she told you Grant? She has moved and lives less than five minutes' walk away from Television Centre.' She did not lose her job, but she received a formal reprimand and was told she would be dismissed if she arrived late for work once more. Why she hadn't told me she now lived a short distance from work when we met prior to the meeting I will never know. That was a definite loss, hey ho.

Personnel Officer Friends

Dick Craig - Tony Trebble - Mary (Dick's wife)

Dick Craig became a close personal friend during my time at the BBC and afterwards (even though he was management and I was a union representative). We both had mutual respect for each other's point of view. Shortly after I retired from the BBC on health grounds my friend Dick came to visit me in my home with his wife Mary and Tony Trebble another close friend. Our friendship continued even when Sue and I moved to Spain on the advice of my orthopaedic consultant after my third spinal operation and we visited Dick and Mary in their holiday villa in Portugal, only a three-hour drive away, for the New Year in 1993. It was a working weekend as Dick roped Sue in to clean the tiles in their swimming pool. On our frequent trips back to the UK we often used to call in to see him and Mary at their home on the south coast. In 2022 when Sue and I were visiting old friends we had not seen for many years, in some cases, thirty to forty, we included a visit to Dick as he was now on our route having moved across the country to a care home nearer his family. He was one hundred years old and in good health and delighted to see us both again. We also kept in touch with Gary Richmond and Tony Trebble for many years by exchanging notes and cards every Christmas. When Tony left the BBC he headed off to Greece where he played the piano in a bar.

Union Officers & Some Friends

Over the years I came into contact and worked closely with a number of ABS union officers, some of whom were close friends, but not all.

Tony Hearn:

Tony Hearn, the General Secretary, and I had an on/off working relationship but I do believe he respected my abilities and I respected his. During his drinking days he could be unpredictable but I shall always remember him as a great negotiator and BBC staff at the time had a lot to thank him for.

Jack Rogers:

As Administration and Finance officer I worked closed with Jack during my lengthy spell as chairman of the A&F committee and as a member of the National Executive Committee. He was a likeable man and easy to get on with, a good organiser when it came to arranging our annual conferences. He shied away from confrontation, hence leaving me to deal with tricky situations when dealing with officer's expenses. Nevertheless, I counted Jack as one of my friends, sadly he died many years ago.

Nick Bunyan:

A likeable rogue who, when you could get hold of him, was easy to deal with. He was responsible for TV1 branch for a while before he then moved on to union members in Transmitters. A friend of sorts.

Tony Banks:

Tony joined the ABS in 1976 and left in 1983. He was responsible for the BBC radio members and a hard worker on their behalf. He did not suffer fools gladly and on occasions when Tony had been drinking too much wine, Tony Banks made him aware of what he thought about it. He was never afraid to speak his mind as he saw it and this was a quality I really enjoyed.

I enjoyed his company and although I was pleased when he went into politics and became a Labour MP for Newham Northwest in 1983 and then progressed to become Minister of Sport, I missed his company at executive meetings. He was created a life peer in 2005 and was known as Baron Stratford but sadly died unexpectedly of a heart attack whilst visiting Florida in the USA in January 2006 at the age of 63. For the brief years I knew Tony, he was indeed a really good friend and a nice down to earth bloke.

Tony Banks and me at Head Office in 1978 joining in the celebration following the initial successful ballot on amalgamation with the ACTT, with Jack Rogers in the background.

Ernie Johnston:

Ernie was a trade union man through and through having been a shop steward at Leyland Motors before he came to the ABS. Ernie got on very well with all the union members wherever he went. He was allocated to be the officer of the Television IBLC in 1977 and we enjoyed a close working relationship. He was a gifted and clever negotiator and not a man who was easily fooled by some of the statistics the BBC management would often throw into the mixing pot. I would definitely say that Ernie was a good friend.

Paddy Leech:

Paddy was the deputy General Secretary but he did not have many dealings with the Television branches although he did come there on occasions.

I usually met him in the BBC Club bar. I only knew him really when attending executive meetings. He was another who liked his drink and could drink a pint of beer in one go, but I never saw him drunk, a capable and reliable officer.

Brian Marsh:

Brian worked with the Television branches and was a likeable officer who got on well with the members. He had a conscientious and methodical approach to the work in hand and was well liked by BBC Management.

Brian and I discussing tactics outside Television Centre 1980.

Mike Marsland:

Mike was the officer responsible for the weekly paid staff and a very likeable and capable officer indeed. Softly spoken but formidable when it came to negotiations with the BBC. As far as Television Centre was concerned Mike dealt mainly with TV6, the weekly paid branch. He always had a cheeky grin whenever you saw him.

Celia Croasdell:

Celia was officer of the Television ILBC for a while and a good officer. She was interested in positive discrimination for women and negotiating for crèche facilities allowing women to return to work. She herself took maternity leave and retuned after the birth of her son Tom. I remember that she had an unfortunate incident when moving into a new home as one day a removal van delivered her belongings and another day burglars brought a van and removed most of her belongings. Sadly, as she was moving to a new area, none of the neighbours realised what was happening.

Christina Driver:

Christina was a hard-working officer who frequently dealt with female members and their particular problems within the workplace, the lack of crèche facilities being only one example.

Doug Smith: The man I was supposed to have tried to murder was an officer I did not get along with. In my personal opinion he was lazy, did little research and could not bring much to the negotiating table, not someone for whom I had a great deal of respect.

John Rickards:

John was not an officer as such, his main role was to assist the Administration & Finance Officer Jack Rogers with his duties, such as arrangements for annual conferences etc. He was polite, softly spoken and a real gentleman, well-liked by those who met him.

John Rickards

Vivian Bellman:

Vivian was a first-class secretary who worked at the ABS office at Television Centre. She was kept busy as her secretarial skills were available to all TV branch representatives who required them. We had a good working relationship spanning several years and are still friends today. Unfortunately she was not the best when it came to parking her car. We would often have a quiet laugh watching her when she arrived for work as the office looked out at the car park.

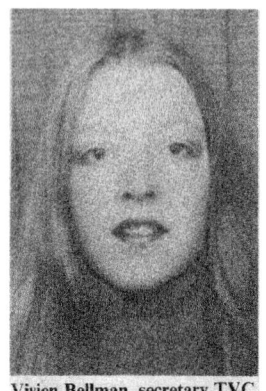

Vivien Bellman, secretary TVC

March in Support of Health Workers

In 1982, on 22nd September, the Television Sub-Divisional Committee organised a march from Television Centre to the green in Shepherds Bush in support of the National Health Workers. It is remarkable that nearly forty years later, after years of conservative neglect, the health unions are still having to strike.

Among those present were: Bill Jenkin (TV5), Simon Higman (TV News), Prue Handley (TV1), Jenny Macarthur (TV4), Melvyn Silverman (TV1), Lorraine Dance (TV1), Brian Marsh (Union Officer), Alan Bowler (Vice President) and me of course.

Apart from being members of the union we were all close friends who got on very well with each other.

Union Moves Offices & Officers Go on Strike

The union moved offices to new and larger premises in Bell Street near the Edgeware Road in 1980 and the following year the union officers went on strike having rejected a pay offer from the national executive. I was vice president at the time and the executive took the decision that the President Eric Stoves, Alan Bowler joint vice president and myself would keep the union ticking over. During the first week the photocopier which we relied on a great deal mysterious broke down and it was our belief that the officers had managed to get one of the clerical staff to do the deed. I went to Tony and suggested that we should send the rest of the staff home so that they could not be put in such a position again. He agreed and that afternoon the remaining staff were sent home until the strike ended.

The officers had a picket line outside the main door that stopped the post from being delivered, but I made arrangements with the post office not to deliver the mail, and I collected it daily from a local office and the officers never caught on. They did have one success when the man from Rank Xerox came to fix the machine and refused to cross the picket line. However, a call to the company and they agreed to send the repair man at six-thirty pm when the pickets had gone to the pub.

There were three pubs in the area, the Constitution, The Perseverance, and the Brazen Head. The officers usually drank in the Perseverance while we chose the Brazen Head. I was rather surprised that quite often Eric Stoves and Alan Bowler would join the officers for a drink and I had my suspicions that they were giving information on how we were coping with running the union on our own.

Meetings were still being arranged with management and with different groups of members and correspondence was maintained albeit at a lower level. Tony Hearn and I worked hard during that period, often staying late at night to get the correspondence done. After nearly a month the executive met and against my advice an increased offer was made It was put forward by the president and was accepted, the strike was over, but some officers held a grudge against me for some time for helping to keep the union afloat.

Amalgamation with NATTKE and another move of Offices

In 1984 after years of talking, the amalgamation with NATTKE who were financially in bad shape finally took place. Initially, the new union was called the ETA (Entertainment Trades Alliance) which comprised the ABS section and the NATTKE section. This merger brought in a further 19,000 union members. John Wilson had been General Secretary of NATTKE since 1975 and he was anxious that the merger took place. Following a Rules Revision Conference the two unions merged completely becoming BETA (Broadcasting and Entertainment Trades' Alliance). New Offices were now required to house all Head Office staff of the amalgamation union and so in 1985 the union moved to Wardour Street in central London. There were two General Secretaries until 1987 when John Wilson retired.

I visited the building on a number of occasions, but to me it was not the same as, out of the 3 Head Offices I had visited, I had much preferred the office in Goodge Street where I had many debates during executive meetings.

BBC Sack 600 Scenic Staff

Another industrial dispute began on 18th February 1984 when the management imposed new conditions of service on staff working in Scenic Services. The staff immediately went on strike and after a couple of days there was only a handful still working. The following week the strike was made official and there were now 540 union members on strike. As the strike dragged on into March it was clear that the management were in no mood for compromise, although they had upped their pay offer to 20%. However, they were determined to reduce the workforce by 160 staff in order to save around one and a half million pounds.

Bill Cotton, the newly appointed Managing Director, sent out letters warning staff they were in breach of their contracts of employment and faced dismissal. A week later, all 600 of those involved were sacked and asked to return their identity cards, a powerful symbol for BBC staff was their BBC Club membership cards. The union response to this was to call on the rest of the staff to support the strikers. This, they had not done so far, Hearn was reported as saying, because they did not want to antagonise the public. Significantly, the other reason he gave for his reluctance to spread the dispute was because of the costs involved. The merged union, which was paying its members strike pay of £30 per week, had spent up until the end of March, £100,000 out of joint funds of £600,000. So on April the 4th, in response to the sacking of the 600 scenery workers, 2,000 staff at Television Centre walked out. BBC management did not attempt to cover for them but allowed the screens to go blank. BBC1 was off the air for 24 hours.

The Rubicon Crossed: This was a signal that times had changed, that the corporation was moving into new territory. The message appeared to get through, on the 9th, both sides met at ACAS and after two days of discussions, the unions recommended acceptance of almost all of the management's demands, in return for an increased pay rise of up to 20% and arbitration in one limited area. The staff reluctantly agreed. Hearn tried to put the best face on it, he told the press the men could go back 'with their heads held high,' but it was a defeat, as the BBC scenery staff returned to work in an atmosphere of tension and bitterness, which was to last months. The balance of power had shifted, and the initiative returned once more to management. It was not merely a question of victors and vanquished though. Both management and unions recognised that the brinkmanship of the recent past would have to be set aside, and there existed a joint understanding of what the problems were and a joint willingness to do something about them.

The End of an Era

As mentioned previously I was becoming more interested in progressing my career within the BBC and when I was not elected as Chairman of the Television Sub-Divisional Committee (I lost by one vote as the member from Milton Keynes arrived just after the vote had been taken due to his train being late), I deemed it a good time to do that. In truth I was not disappointed having been chairman for seven years and serving on the committee as vice-chairman for two years, definitely time for a change. I had been elected at the 1984 Annual Council to the national executive and was Vice President. I returned to the Gramophone Library to resume my duties as AIC and immediately began to enjoy working there full-time with the occasional meeting dealing with TV7, the managerial branch. However, after three months I received a call from Ian Marshall saying that I had been head-hunted for a position at Lime Grove.

I thought it over and decided that it was worth a go but I insisted that if it did not work out then I would return to the Gramophone library.

Lime Grove Studios

I went to Lime Grove Television Studios and met with the Personnel Officer John ? (surname escapes me) who assured me that I was the man to reorganise the work and increase productivity of the Film Department at Lime Grove, and that I would have my own secretary. When I walked into the department you could have heard a pin drop, the other managers present of course knew me as a trade union representative who in their opinion had done damage to the department. I introduced myself, outlined my new role and when I asked for any comments, not a word was spoken. Undeterred I set about going through the files and held meetings with other members of staff ascertaining their views as to how we could improve things within the department for everyone's benefit.

After a month, no secretary had arrived and the other managers were still giving me the cold shoulder. However, undeterred, I set about making a detailed report (typing it myself) of proposed changes that would increase productivity within the department. It was several thousand words and several pages in length when I concluded it. It was two months to the day when I handed it in and I immediately returned to the Gramophone Library as AIC.

Final Gift to the Gramophone Library

I had been working on a project over the past few months as there was no definite information in one specific place on classical composers from the second to the twentieth century showing their country of origin and the dates of birth and death. This information would be useful for productions and other gramophone libraries.

I was determined to get it completed and spent many hours including after work (not getting paid overtime) ensuring that all of the details were correct before I had the book printed. Copies were sent to all BBC libraries who were grateful to add it to their stock.

Classical Composers
Country of Origin

From 2nd to 20th Century

Grant Bremner

AIC
Televison Gramophone Library

Dresser Manager

In the summer of 1984 Costume Department created a new post of Dresser Manager, it being long overdue. There were one hundred and ninety-four full time dressers in the department plus around forty others on short term-contracts to cover the busiest period during the summer and annual leave of course. I applied for the post and was duly interviewed by Maggie McPherson, Head of Costume Department, and Roger Reece, her deputy, and I was delighted that Duncan Thomas Personnel Officer for Design Group was not present although I was to learn later that he had given instructions that I was not to be appointed to the post. However, Maggie and Roger thankfully did not take his advice and I was appointed as Dresser Manager. At the interview I informed them that there was one union personal case in which I was still involved and that I wanted them to know about it as I was going to see it through because it involved an Industrial Tribunal.

The Gramophone Library was located on the third floor of Television Centre in room 3044 and my new office was room 3016 just along the corridor. I already knew many of the costume designers and assistant designers having managed their grading claim as chairman of TV1 branch, so when I eventually took up my new post three months later I was welcomed with open arms. Music and Arts department would not let me go to my new position as they did not know what to do about my replacement.

In the end they were forced to as one evening with two members of the costume allocation team responsible for dressers off sick an urgent situation had arisen and Barbara Kronig, a Senior Costume Designer, came and asked if I could help. We both stayed until late that night, but we got the job done. The following day I demanded that Music and Arts release me immediately, which they did. Not being able to decide who should replace me as AIC Gramophone Library, Music & Arts ducked the issue by sharing the post for six months each between my deputy Melvyn Silverman and Richard Pope. Why Melvyn allowed this to happen I do not know but I was powerless to help him.

I had been allocated a secretary by Costume Department, but she only lasted two weeks. I had given her quite a lot of dictation during that time, so I could only assume that it was the workload she was not happy with. However, that gave me the opportunity to look for a new secretary myself and I interviewed a few prospective candidates and then settled on a lady I knew instantly I could get on well with, her name Gill Berido. Every member of staff has an annual report that assesses their work over the past year (some higher paid managers are excluded) and of course none of my dressers had ever had one, so I set about the task with gusto.

I spoke to costume designers and their assistants about the work of the dressers they had been allocated on their productions and the allocations staff. I made copious notes then dictated the report on the individuals concerned to Gill who typed them up.

Once completed and signed by me I asked Gill to arrange for the dresser to come to see me for their annual assessment and interview. You can imagine, with one hundred and ninety plus to deal with, this endeavour consumed a great deal of my time, and I often found myself working late. (MP2 staff did not get paid overtime).

As dresser manager I would go down to the various studios on a regular basis to talk with members of my staff and of course any of the artists who would be performing in front of the cameras as well as the costume designers. There was always a good atmosphere here, although on some occasions a little tense as artists had of course to remember their lines and could be rather nervous. This way I met a lot of remarkably interesting artists, and one in particular that became a friend, Bella Emberg who played Blunder Woman on the Russ Abbott Show. She had asked me very politely if she could have the same dresser, with whom she got on so well, for the current and next series, a request I was most happy to grant.

On one occasion when the programme Tripods was shooting at an outside location near my home in Hazlemere I took Sue along with me so she could see how it was put together. No sooner had we arrived on location when a costume designer rushed up and asked me if Sue would be willing to be a dresser for the day as there were many children to dress as part of a circus audience and they were short of staff. Sue readily agreed to help out and I do believe she thoroughly enjoyed herself as did I talking to my staff.

On another occasion I visited an outside location while an episode of Miss Marple was being filmed. What a gentle and amenable star Joan Hickson was. It was in the winter and she patiently waited in the car for her scene to be shot while dressers bustled round giving her blankets and hot water bottles to keep her warm.

A few of the many Artists I've come across:

David Attenborough - Andy Stewart - Shirley Bassey - Rory Bremner - Russ Abbott - Bella Emberg - Ronnie Corbett - Ronnie Barker (The Two Ronnies), Joan Hickson (Miss Marple), Spike Milligan - Bruce Forsyth - Harry Secombe - Noel Edmonds - Harry H Corbett, Wilfred Bramble (Steptoe & Son) - Felicity Kendal, Richard Briers, Penelope Keith (The Good, Life) - Patrick Moore (The Sky at Night) - Warren Mitchell, Una Stubbs, Dandy Nichols (Till Death Us Do Part) - Les Dawson – Lenny Henry – Bill Oddie, Tim Brooke Taylor, Graham Garden (The Goodies) - Rik Mayall, Ade Edmondson, Nigel Planer, Ben Elton, Jennifer Saunders (The Young Ones).

There were of course many more artists that I saw either in a studio or in the BBC Club during my many years at Television Centre. Many pop stars such as Cliff Richard & The Shadows, The Beatles, The Rolling Stones, The Kinks, The Animals, The Dave Clark Five, The Who, Herman's Hermits, Manfred Mann, The Moody Blues, The Searchers, Gerry & The Pacemakers, Procol Harum, The Small Faces, Freddy Mercury & Queen, all had regular appearances during the sixties and seventies on Top of the Pops which was recorded in different studios.
Some of the Individual singers I recall who appeared on Top of the Pops were: Elton John, David Bowie, Sandie Shaw, Dusty Springfield, Tom Jones, Olivia Newton John, Kate Bush, Rod Stewart, Joe Cocker, Cat Stevens, Peter Gabriel, Cilla Black, Lulu, and many more.

I have seen microphones being thrown across the studio in a temper, artists losing their cool, having a tantrum and shouting at members of staff when lines were forgotten or just fluffed. However, that said being in a studio environment in front of a television camera can be stressful even for a hardened actor or singer and in the end they always gave of their very best.

BBC Friends

I must admit it was good to be back in Television Centre doing a job I thoroughly enjoyed, Lime Grove had been a disaster, but not of my making. As the manager of well over two hundred and forty dressers, both permanent and casual staff there was plenty to keep me occupied, and it was also nice to be back with good friends at work.

John Woolmer was a video tape engineer and a member of TV2 branch and he was also on the executive committee for a number of years as well as a member of the Television Sub-Divisional Committee.

His partner, **Heta**, worked in PABX and I remember an incident when a fairly new personnel officer from Central Services called her to go behind the working area where she asked for her ID card saying that she had bounced a cheque and that cashing facilities had now been withdrawn. She then proceeded to punch a hole through the ID card before handing it back. The staff who were working that day were of course privy to the conversation.

PABX Television Centre

That afternoon Heta came to see me and provided proof that she had not bounced a cheque, so I took the matter up with Steve Ansell the chief personnel officer for that area. I informed him that what had occurred was indeed a grave error and should not have taken place in a public space. I added that an immediate apology was required in the PABX area in front of the staff. I also asked that her card should be restored forthwith. I further stated that if it did not happen today then TV1 branch would withdraw from all future meetings with Central Services. Heta was most pleased with the outcome later that afternoon.

John was also an excellent cook and he loved doing a proper Chinese Banquet at the Chinese New Year. He once made a seven-course meal for us which was delicious, although we did not manage to eat all of the courses. When he retired he and Heta moved to Tenerife in the Canary Islands.

Eileen Mair was a senior Make-up artist when I first met her during the grading claim for Make-up artists. She had an amazing list of productions that she had worked on over the years, and she was sought after by television producers and artists alike. We became close friends and would on occasions have a sandwich and a drink in the BBC Club at lunch time. Before I retired I was delighted when she became Head of Make-up Department, a well-deserved appointment and not before time. For many years she did the Queen's make-up prior to her Christmas Speech.

Melvyn Silverman: Sadly I have not got a decent photograph of Melvyn (although he features in a couple of photos in this book). Apart from being a union colleague Melvyn was a good friend over many years. We worked in the Television Gramophone Library together and a special bond had developed between us. Ronnie Hazlehurst wrote many themes for BBC Television Programmes including: Are You Being Served; Some Mothers Do 'Ave 'Em; Last of the Summer Wine; I Didn't Know You Cared; The Fall and Rise of Reginald Perrin; To the Manor Born; Yes, Minister; Yes, Prime Minister; Just Good Friends. Well, Ronnie always insisted on dealing with Melvyn to help him with his music requests and got rather annoyed if he was on holiday when he had to deal with me for his musical needs. Sadly Melvyn died at the age of 42 from cancer, gone but never forgotten.

Prue Handley was a senior Costume Designer and a member of TV1 branch for many years. She was also the first female chairman of the branch. She worked on many large productions showing her skill as a costume designer, and she was of course eagerly sought after by productions and artists alike. She was a useful asset to the branch committee, she spoke her mind freely and did not suffer fools gladly. We are still in contact via annual Christmas cards. She now lives in Norfolk with her husband Alan.

I wrote the following in ABStract in 1984:

Prue Handley has escaped

Prue Handley has left the BBC to join Anglia Television. She has left behind many friends and colleagues who will miss her formidable style of negotiation, although I can think of a number of people who hold managerial positions who will not bewail her departure for too long.

Prue was the first woman chairman of TV1 branch. She joined the BBC in 1973 having spent many years working for ATV. As a costume designer she was well respected by the staff within the production departments for the total commitment she brought to the programme. She won the BAFTA award for her costumes on the television production of Testament of Youth in 1981, an award which recognise her undoubted skill as a costume designer. Although Prue was an active member of the ABS, her first and foremost considerations were always for the well-being of costume department. If I were to try and list her achievements as a union representative over the years it would be a formidable one indeed. Many members have cause to remember Prue with gratitude as she took a keen and active interest in all the various activities with which the branch committee were dealing during her period of office. She was chairman of the branch for three years and vice-chairman during her last six months. Prue and I attended countless meetings with differing managements over the years and I cannot recall one single meeting when she was not prepared either by having the appropriate file or by being well versed on the particular matter before us.

On behalf of her friends, colleagues and acquaintances (including some from management) I would like to take this opportunity of expressing our sincere thanks and appreciation to Prue and to wish her every success at Anglia Television.

W. Grant Bremner.

Barbara Kronig was also a Senior Costume Designer who I got to know very well during my time as Dresser Manager. Barbara was totally committed to the department and without her steady hand at the helm it would not have been as successful as it was. She possessed an in-depth knowledge of all costume designers and when it came to allocations to productions she was spot on. In my opinion she should have been made the Head of the Department after Maggie McPherson's departure. A true and loyal friend.

Avril Standing worked in the administration office in Costume Department and she knew almost everyone who worked in the department. She was always smiling at work and as we both usually arrived early for work we would have a coffee in my office and put the world to rights, including Costume Department. She and Gill my secretary became good friends.

Dinner prior to my retirement

Joe (Gill's husband) - Gill - Me - Avril - Sue

There are of course many more good friends that I met during my thirty years with the BBC and here are some of their names (in no particular order):

Bill Jenkin - Roger Bolton - John Barlow - Jenny Macarthur - Barry Luckhurst - John Elfes - John Walbeof - John Gray - Don Horn - Roy Davis - John Armstrong - Chic Anthony - Mike Hollingworth - Lorraine Dance - Jean Steward - Eileen Mair - Barbara Kronig - Bob Springett - Gerry Beasley - Lynn Bracewell - Melvyn Silverman - Prue Handley - Dinah Walker - Ian Marshall - The Graphics Design Team - Kate McDonald - Margaret Butcher.

I would also like to thank the many people who served on TV1 branch committee over the years, without your dedicated support the branch would not have been as successful as it was.

25 Year Service Award

On 18th January 1985 I had completed 25 years' service working for the BBC, and I was invited to meet with Duncan Thomas in his office. When I arrived there I was rather surprised to see Maggie McPherson also present, obviously Duncan did not want to meet me on my own. I noted he had my personnel file on his desk which he obviously had gone through. His secretary came in with a tray and three glasses of Champagne offering a glass to each of us.

'I see you were earning £3.14 shillings when you started working for us Grant, I guess you're earning a bit more now, here's your twenty-five year cheque.' I was amazed that was all Duncan had to say about my twenty-five years' service. That was the custom back then, a month's salary if you completed twenty-five years. We all drank the glass of Champagne quickly and that was the end of the conversation with Mr. Thomas. On the way out his secretary handed me the bottle of champagne and Maggie and I walked back to my office where we finished the bottle together with Gill my secretary.

Back Problems Begin

Charing Cross Hospital

In July 1985, an old friend from my music days in the Gramophone Library came to take me out to lunch. As I got up from my chair to extend my hand to greet him, suddenly my back went into what I can only call a severe painful spasm, and instead of lunch I was taken to Charing Cross Hospital where I was to spend the following three months in the south wing on the seventh floor - 7 South. This wing together with 7 West, made up the orthopaedic department on the seventh floor, comprising wards varying from 6 or 4 occupants down to single rooms. On examination in the A&E department the registrar said he had never seen a back in such rigid spasm and it was to remain that way for several weeks. They did many tests starting with a myelogram, injecting dye into the spinal canal. Of course, these days MRIs have made myelograms relatively obsolete, a pity they weren't available in the 80s!! I had previously had a myelogram a couple of years before when the severe reaction to the dye turned my expected one overnight stay into more than a week which meant they had to move me out of the 5 day ward I was in. However, the myelogram in 1985 caused no such problems (apparently they used a water-based rather than an oil-based dye). I was confined to bed for many weeks while they tried various procedures rather than operating. First, they tried traction by putting weights on my legs, in an attempt to stretch the muscles free I assume, this lasted two weeks. Thursdays became my theatre day of the week firstly when I was sent there after traction had not worked for manipulation under anaesthetic but they were unable to proceed with manipulation as the back spasm was too acute. The next Thursday it was a radiculogram with the following week being spinal anaesthetic which they did not give opting for manipulation this time. This was unsuccessful and with no success with anything they tried, a decision was taken to operate on my back the following week. However, fate intervened. I became extremely ill with severe sickness and diarrhoea and, within a few days, I had lost over a stone in weight. I was now too ill to have an operation. It was Sue who suggested (quite forcefully) to the Staff Nurse that perhaps they should call in a gastroenterologist to examine me and my medicine chart.

Going through the chart thoroughly he spotted the error immediately, a strong painkiller called Ponstan that I had been put on when I first arrived. Apparently it should have been given to me for no longer than fourteen days. Obviously they stopped giving me the painkiller immediately, but it took me another two weeks before I was to recover enough strength to undergo an operation and then the kitchens in the hospital were closed down due to an infestation of cockroaches. My junior registrar told me that if I saw a cockroach on my plate I should eat it as it contained a lot of protein!! His name was David Anderson and he was a great joker and proved a huge asset in the times to come.

By the time I was well enough for the operation my consultant, Mr Strachan, had gone on holiday to Scotland for a fortnight (fishing I seem to remember) and during that time a new registrar thought it would be a clever idea to have me exercise in the hospital heated hydro pool. I personally did not think that it was a good idea but nevertheless he ordered daily hydrotherapy sessions. I had had 2 sessions in the pool, a Friday and a Monday (luckily the pool was closed at weekends) before thankfully Mr Strachan arrived, just as I was about to undress to get into the pool the following day. I don't know who told him, but he was back from holiday and had come straight down to the hydro pool. He examined me, then instructed them to take me back to the ward, he was going to operate on me 2 days later, the Thursday of that week.

During the operation they found that a piece of the disc had broken away and was trapped against the nerve, hence the pain and the severe spasm. Mr Strachan performed a fenestration discectomy, cutting and removing a piece of the disc which was pushing against the nerve and thus allowing the nerve to move freely. The following day David Anderson came and said I had to get up and move around. After 9 weeks of little movement and severe gastric problems I was very weak so, rugby player that he was, David put his arm around me and, with my feet only just touching the floor, helped me to take some exercise.

I continued to exercise every day and 10 days later, once the stitches were out, started hydrotherapy. Finally, after 11 weeks in hospital I was thrilled to be allowed home for the weekend before returning on the Monday for more intensive hydrotherapy. As Sue drove me home I realised just how long I had been away as all the trees were now changing colour with the onset of autumn. A couple more weeks of inpatient hydrotherapy and I was discharged. To be perfectly honest, despite the time it took to diagnose the problem, I was glad it had been discovered and that I'd soon be back to work, three months away is a long time.

During that length of time I saw quite a few patients who were much worse off than me. There was one man who had been in a horrific road traffic accident, he had about a dozen pins through both legs, plaster on both arms and yet he was a really cheerful bloke. There was a man who exercised in the hydro pool who had been pinned all the way up his spine as disc after disc began to deteriorate. In contrast there was a young chap in the bed next to me for a couple of days who had hurt his knee. After tests and a visit from the physiotherapist he was discharged, something he was not happy about as he was enjoying having his 3 girlfriends visiting him with various gifts of food and chocolate. He was living dangerously though and was lucky that they didn't bump into each other, although it was close on one occasion when one arrived shortly after another had left - they must have passed somewhere in the hospital.

Many of the staff in Costume Department came to visit while I was in hospital, and they even had a collection to buy me a gift. Barbara Kronig handed me a portable cassette player and a couple of music tapes. 'We thought this would help to relieve the boredom Grant,' she said with an engaging smile and it certainly did. There was a hospital radio programme, and the volunteers would come around the wards and ask patients what music we would like played on the radio. 'Also Sprach Zarathustra by Richard Strauss,' I said cheekily. 'Can you spell it?' she asked, which I did and the following day she returned to tell me that unfortunately they couldn't find it in their small record library. She wasn't aware that I was only joking. I also won a big box of chocolates for guessing the score in a cricket match, apparently I was the closest by one run.

When I was eventually discharged I was told to rest for at least a month in order to allow the wound and muscles they had cut through to heal properly.

In the event I went back to my job as Dresser manager after two weeks as I was well aware that the Head of Costume Department Maggie McPherson and her deputy Roger Reece were not best pleased that I had been absent for three months. In retrospect, it was a bad decision health-wise to return so soon to work as it was not long before the pain in my back returned but I managed to cope with it somehow.

Industrial Tribunal

Back as Dresser Manager I got to work clearing up the back log of annual reports, I had almost completed them all and had also conducted a series of interviews for thirty plus contract dressers to cover the next busy summer period ahead. Then news came that the personal case I had mentioned was to be heard at an Industrial Tribunal meeting. The person concerned was George Thain who had been a union member and a Scenic Artist prior to his dismissal from the BBC. George had got into a fight with another member of staff in the office of the acting manager and both had been dismissed the same day on the instructions of Duncan Thomas, Head of Design Group. The altercation had begun in the Scenic Artists studio and the acting manager had called them both into a very small office with no room for chairs, so they had stood right next to each other. It had been my contention that the manager should have separated them and then spoken to them individually allowing the situation to calm down. Instead he brought them both into the tiny office and the altercation began once more. Before the tribunal had begun I got a copy of the blueprint of the office, showing that it measured only 7ft by 5ft with a desk and a chair occupied by the acting manager who had no experience, this was his first day acting in the post. Duncan Thomas along with Hans Norton from Industrial Relations were both there watching and listening to me giving evidence on George's behalf as to why he should not have been dismissed so quickly after almost twenty years of exemplary service to the BBC.

The tribunal lasted most of the day and said it would render its decision within two weeks. When the result came through from the tribunal the BBC were instructed to reinstate George Thain with full pay and benefit rights maintained. However, tribunals are only advisory, so the BBC dug their heels in and refused to reinstate him, he did however retain his full pension rights. As far as Duncan Thomas was concerned that was another nail in my coffin, I'd beaten him yet again.

Sad Events

I was really enjoying my role as Dresser Manager, annual reports were up to date and I held regular meetings with the dressers and held several induction meetings with new contract staff informing them of how the BBC operated and what was expected of them now that they were an employee of the BBC, albeit on contract. Then unfortunately some dressers started to make false expense claims when they were on location at Elstree Studios working on EastEnders. The matter was brought to my attention by the costume finance manager Bob Brown, but the claims in question were in doubt due to the lack of proof. I sent a memo to all of the dressers informing them that claiming overnight expenses when they had actually returned home was fraud and would not be tolerated. I also held several staff meetings to that effect.

Prior to EastEnders starting transmission I had visited Elstree Studios in order to establish the dressers' work area and was now disappointed at this news.

After approximately one month had passed, a costume designer working on EastEnders at Elstree Film Studios came to see me and informed me that she was absolutely certain that some dressers were going home each night, but they were claiming their overnight expenses. The only way to prove that they were doing this was to get a BBC inspector to visit the hotel after they had submitted their expenses to enquire if they had actually been there. Dick Gray, the personnel officer responsible, arranged this and we both received a written report along with copies of the expense claim forms, none of the staff who had claimed an overnight allowance had stayed overnight. The amount of money in question was not a great deal, but each fraudulent claim was over three hundred pounds.

The three staff members concerned were asked to come to an interview with myself and Dick Gray, as this was a fact-finding interview it had not been necessary to inform TV1 branch. Only two members of staff turned up for their interview the other one had called in sick. Both were asked to explain their expense claims and asked the question had they stayed where they had claimed, I asked each to be truthful in their response.

Unfortunately, they chose to maintain they had stayed at the hotel in question. They were then informed that we had written evidence to the contrary and Dick Gray asked them to go home and informed them that they would receive a letter asking them to come to a formal meeting at which they could be represented by a union member or a friend. Had they been truthful and admitted they hadn't stayed, another interview may not have been necessary, but they had both insisted they had stayed at the hotel in Elstree during the nights in question.

Further investigations were held regarding the older claims and we received confirmation that the practice had been widespread at Elstree for some time. Although Elstree Film Studio was only 13 miles from Television Centre, staff were allowed to stay overnight locally in order for them to be on site early the following morning. Letters were sent to the three members of staff involved asking them to attend a formal meeting and informing them they could have a union representative present, only one chose to do so. It was with deep regret that following the interviews there was no alternative but to sack the three individuals concerned. I am sure we could have been more lenient if only they had owned up during the initial interview. I was certainly not proud of my part in this, but I had warned my staff in writing and verbally about the consequences if anyone knowingly submitted a false expense claim.

Looking back at the situation I wondered if there had been anything else I could have done that would have resulted in them being able to keep their jobs and I concluded that as their manager I had done my very best in warning them of the severe consequences of fraudulent claims.

Back into Hospital

In February 1987 less than eighteen months after my spinal operation I once again went into severe spasm while at work and the BBC doctor immediately sent me by taxi to Mr. Strachan's private consulting rooms in Harley Street. He examined me, then I had an x-ray on the premises and within an hour I was back in the orthopaedic wing 7 South in Charing Cross Hospital. This time I was in for a week initially having a discogram in the theatre and a series of dye tests, after which I was allowed home for 10 days before returning for a scheduled operation. On this occasion it was a double fusion with four stainless steel screws inserted to keep the discs stable. I required a blood transfusion after the operation and someone actually gave me the wrong blood type. Sue was visiting at the time thankfully and she noticed that I was beginning to look poorly, so she brought this to the attention of a nurse who checked the blood bag attached to my arm and realised there had been a mistake. I dread to think what might have happened had Sue not been there. I was in there for 3 weeks this time in a bay with four beds and I think that bay of Ward 7 must have been jinxed. A man delirious with anaesthetic following a hip operation tried to set his bed on fire with a match. Another man in the bed next to me (who was only in the orthopaedic wing because they had no bed for him elsewhere) haemorrhaged while his family were at his bedside, and he died almost immediately. Because I'd seen it happen, the nurses decided to give me a quiet room for the night, so they put me in the only available space - a storage room, with a skeleton - true.

Before being discharged from the hospital my consultant Mr. Strachan insisted that when the fusion had taken hold properly and the muscles had healed he would call me back into hospital for hydrotherapy and that on this occasion I must take at least 4 months off work to allow my body to heal.

Roger Reece came to see me at my home in April and he made it clear that my prolonged absence from my post through ill health was not going down well, so the following week I went to see the BBC doctor John Newman and we discussed my problem. Given my consultant's instructions and his own examination he refused to sign me off sick leave confirming that I was not yet fit for work.

Throughout June I went back to the hospital for hydrotherapy sessions several times a week and by the beginning of July I was allowed to return to work as both

Mr. Strachan and John Newman assessed me as fit enough. (Sadly, this second operation proved to be unsuccessful and 4 months later I was back in Charing Cross Hospital for manipulation under anaesthetic with Mr. Strachan.)

When I did return to work I was greeted by grumblings within Costume Department amongst Senior Costume Designers and designers often upset by the way Roger Reece was managing the department and in particular his apparent favours when allocating certain designers to programmes. He was autocratic in his dealings with staff, did not listen to their complaints and there was general unrest throughout the department. A report was commissioned on the running of the department and interviews were held with staff and all managers including myself, plus many other staff members. This lasted several weeks and it was a couple of months before we heard the news that Roger Reece had been sent home. He was not a union member, but I telephoned him at home and told him to resist any deal the BBC may initially offer. In the end he chose to accept what was offered and we never again heard from him.

Work then carried on as normal until, about three months after Roger's departure, Maggie McPherson came to see me on a personal matter and informed me that she had been instructed to go home by Duncan Thomas as her services were no longer required. I was aware that she was not a union member, but the manner in which she was about to be dismissed without any recourse was something that I could not and would not tolerate. I told her I would represent her as her friend and I rang and demanded a meeting with Duncan Thomas and to my surprise he agreed. I opened the meeting with Maggie present by telling Mr. Thomas I was there as her friend as allowed for in the staff instructions. I asked if she had ever received any informal or formal warning regarding her shortcomings as manager either verbally, in writing or at an annual interview.

Duncan replied that he did not write annual reports on senior management. I asked why not as conditions of service stated that all members of staff were entitled to an annual report and that there were no exclusions for MP staff. He replied that he had verbally spoken of her shortcomings as a manager to which Maggie said vehemently he was a liar. The meeting concluded with me informing Mr Thomas that Maggie was returning to her post until such time as formal disciplinary proceedings as detailed within the agreed staff instructions were started against her and that any perceived failings should be put in writing.

Back in my office I made it clear to Maggie that it was obvious that her position within Costume Department was now untenable. I would go and see Roger Chase who was now the BBC Director of Personnel working at Broadcasting House. I met with Roger the following day and we enjoyed a bite to eat and a glass of wine together, it was lunch time. In discussing Maggie's position we both agreed she would have no option but to leave Costume department.

'Tell her to come back to Personnel Grant, I'll find her a job.' I gave Maggie the message from Roger and she left Costume Department the following week and started working at Broadcasting House. Another nail in my coffin having thwarted Duncan Thomas yet again.

Jill Shardlow was appointed Head of Costume Department following Maggie's departure and a close Make-up friend of mine Eileen Mair was appointed as Head of Make-up Department.

Eileen was an extremely talented make-up artist who went to Buckingham Palace for many years to do the Queen's make-up prior to the recording of her Christmas speech to the nation. Her Majesty always asked for Eileen as they got on well together. Eileen was well liked by the hundreds of production staff she had worked with over the years, and she had become a really good friend that I could talk to and relax with. She worked on major productions such as The Onedin Line, Survivors, Blakes Seven, Anthony & Cleopatra and The Taming of the Shrew, these being just a few examples.

Work carried on as normal and I thought I had a decent working relationship with the new head of the department until one Monday evening in March around seven o'clock when I had quite a heavy cold Jill Shardlow noticed this and told me to go home. I did as instructed and stayed home for the remainder of the week. I did get a sick note from my doctor and handed it in on my return and thought no more about it. A couple of weeks later I returned to my office having just completed an induction seminar for new contract dressers when my secretary informed me that Dick Gray, my personnel officer, had left an envelope on my desk. On opening the letter I was amazed to read that I had been deducted four days pay for being off sick. It went on to say that any sickness in future may lead to my termination of service with the BBC.

There were a number of issues with the letter: firstly, all staff must be warned first verbally about excessive sickness, and then formally in writing, and any deductions of salary again had to be notified in advance.

I was so angry that I immediately rang Dick Gray and told him that he was a ******* coward, sneaking into my office when he knew I was not there and leaving a letter on my desk. Instantly I regretted my choice of words, swearing at a personnel officer could have led to instant dismissal. He asked if I could meet him in the BBC club at lunchtime which I agreed to. Surprisingly, when he got there it was he who apologised to me when we met as he was well aware that he had not complied with conditions of service and that I could take the matter further if I chose. However, I decided against this course of action as it would only highlight the times I had been off in hospital.

It was my belief that he had been acting on the instructions of Duncan Thomas as he was well aware that he should have spoken to me long before he dropped off the letter in my office. He bought me a drink and we did not discuss my sick leave any more. I knew then that my career with the BBC was coming to an end, it was only a matter of time as my back continued to give me a lot of pain and there was bound to be another time when I would be unable to come to work.

I continued working to the best of my ability but matters came to a head when severe back pain returned again in May the following year 1988. Towards the end of the month I went to discuss the problem with John Newman the BBC doctor who after a fairly lengthy discussion told me that my best course of action would be to retire on health grounds which he would support as it was clear I had a continuing back problem.

It had been my intention to inform Jill Shardlow of this, but when I went to see her in her office her secretary told me she had gone on holiday and would be away for the whole of June. To be completely honest I was utterly amazed that she had gone off without telling the Dresser Manager that she would be away, we usually met each Monday morning to discuss any matters of interest within the department. I carried on work as normal and then the week before she was due to return I contacted John Newman and arranged to meet with him at 11am on the day Jill returned from holiday.

When Monday arrived I went to see John at the agreed time only to discover he had been called away on duty. I asked his secretary to call me the moment he returned. I did not want to mention anything to Jill until I had confirmation from John that I could go home. It had gone noon when I saw him, and he officially instructed me to go home as he was going to start the retirement procedure on health grounds immediately. The first person I told was my secretary Gill who broke into tears at the news and I genuinely felt sad at that moment. After a few minutes I walked into Jill's office and informed her of the decision of the BBC doctor, she was shocked at the news. During the month she'd been away on holiday I had removed all of my personal belongs from my office, something Gill had noticed and realised something was up. She waved to me when I turned round at the main entrance to look at my office on the third floor for the last time as a working employee of the BBC, I had tears in my eyes as I waved back. I did not return to Television Centre until 12th January 1989 for my retirement party.

My Retirement Party

> *Jill Shardlow*
> *Head of Costume Department, Television*
> *requests the pleasure of the company of*
>
> ....
>
> *at a party in 1257, Television Centre,*
> *Wood Lane W12*
> *to mark the retirement of*
> *Grant Bremner*
> *on Thursday, January 12th 1989*
>
> 6.00 – 9.30   R.S.V.P. to
> Dress informal   Gill Berido
>   Room 3015 T.C.
>   Tel: 01 576 1716

So it was that Sue and I took the train and tube to White City and we walked back into Television Centre after six months. I can't remember how many people were invited but a lot of my BBC & union friends were there to greet me. Roger Johnson from personnel presented me with a retirement gift, a Psion Organiser II, and Sue was presented with a beautiful bunch of flowers.

Photographs From the Occasion

The Flowers

Roger Johnson - Dick Craig - Tony Trebble

Eileen Mair Head of Make-Up Department,
my best friend and confidant over the years.

Heather - Dinah - Jean - Maggie - Isabelle - Penny

Team from Graphics Design

Brian - Brian - Alastair - Keith - Bernard

Heather - Jean (and her husband) - Maggie - Gary

Jack - Bob - Avril - Ernie

Joe & Gill Berido (my loyal secretary) - Me

Bill Marshall - Judy Allan - John Newman (BBC Doctor) - Ian from personnel

John - Kate - John (First man to black film)

Prue - Dick - Tony

Eileen - Me - Lorraine - Mike

The party is over and we adjourned to the BBC Club for a final drink and some reminiscing together of the good times we enjoyed.

I consider myself to have been very fortunate to have worked for the BBC for almost 30 years, from my humble beginnings as Office Junior in Aberdeen to Dresser Manager in Television Centre. To have experienced all that I have in those creative years was indeed a privilege and I extend my sincere thanks to all those with whom I came into contact during that time, both in the BBC and in the union, who helped to make my life in the BBC such an extraordinary one.

Thank You from Director General Mike Checkland:

BBC

FROM THE DIRECTOR-GENERAL

BRITISH BROADCASTING CORPORATION
BROADCASTING HOUSE
LONDON W1A 1AA
TELEPHONE: 01-580 4468
TELEGRAMS AND CABLES: BROADCASTS LONDON
TELEX: 265781

3rd January 1989

Dear Grant,

I am writing on the occasion of your retirement to thank you for all you have done for the BBC over the last twenty-eight years.

Throughout your career, your commitment to your BBC work and your involvement in Industrial Relations on behalf of the ABS and more recently the BETA have been greatly appreciated.

The majority of your time with the BBC was, of course, spent in the Gramophone Library, and your contribution to the development of this area will be invaluable to subsequent Library staff. In recent years you have been the first Dresser Manager in Costume Department and the innovations that you have initiated have undoubtedly improved the efficiency of this important service to programme-makers.

I am sorry that your back problems have made it necessary for you to be retired prematurely, and I send you my best wishes for a long and happy retirement.

Yours sincerely,

Michael Checkland

Mr. W.G. Bremner,
14 Pine Walk,
Hazlemere,
Bucks.
HP15 7TR

Farewell to the BBC:

Page 12 — *Ariel, January 17 1989*

Farewell

Alan Davies

If Alan Davies hadn't joined the RAF in 1942 he would have been a professional footballer.

Alan was trained in the Air Force as an engine fitter and flew in many sorts of aeroplane in photographic work and supply dropping. He was stationed for years during the war in the Middle and Far East in the 357AC or, as it was later named, Lord Mountbatten's 'Forgotten Army'. He saw most of India but sadly never managed a visual on the Taj Mahal.

When Alan was demobbed in 1948 he went into the manufacture of ladies underwear, mostly making brassieres. He swears the motto of the company was 'we can make mountains out of molehills' — but then one can never be too sure when Alan is being serious.

He changed his trade to a new venture when he went into a leather goods business, and I can well remember when he proudly showed him a brand new pair of shiny black tap dancing shoes and, after the briefest of examinations, he pointed to the toe and said they were flawed. Sure enough, six months later a split appeared exactly where Alan had stated there was a problem.

Fifteen years ago Alan joined the Maintenance staff at Research Department and after a year asked to go to the specialist area of Workshops, where he has been ever since. He is liked by everyone and but wit and especially his wonderful stories and jokes will be sorely missed by one and all, as will his enthusiasm to make a first class job of everything he undertakes. *David Bishop.*

John Wootton

After more than 25 years loyal service, John Wootton is retiring from the BBC. Having spent ten years in the Engineering Department of the Royal Free Hospital, John joined the BBC as a fitter, class I in 1963.

Initially based at Television Centre, he moved to Lime Grove after two years. In 1959 he was highly commended for the part he played in controlling and repairing damage caused by severe flooding at Golders Green Hippodrome.

John returned to Television Centre in 1988, but despite strenuous efforts on his part, was regrettably forced to retire early due to ill health.

His quiet-spoken friendly personality will be missed by all who had the pleasure to know and work with him.

We all wish John and his wife a long and happy retirement. *B D Doherty.*

Robin Wylie

After almost 27 years of service in BBC Northern Ireland, Robin Wylie is taking early retirement.

After a period of casual and contract employment as a designer and as a floor manager, Robin joined the staff in 1963. He then began a steady rise through the ranks until, in 1975, he was appointed as a Television producer in Northern Ireland. This was the culmination of much distinguished work as a PA during an exceedingly difficult period for the Corporation in Belfast, as it came to grips with the unfolding sectarian conflict.

Robin played no small part in defining the responsibilities of the region's nightly news magazine during this period, but he also found time to develop his skills in relation to the discipline which would become his first love — film-making!

Robin's work was noted for its creativity and authority, its quality soon recognised by network controllers who were pleased to place in their schedules such films as Surgery of Violence and The Move, and to feature his work in strands such as Man Alive, Network and The Irish Way. On the local front his series provide a unique record of the life and work of some major figures in Irish society.

Robin's departure from the BBC does not mean that his creative life is over. Indeed, he still has much to contribute through the television screen and through the canvas (another great love) to the creation of a full and honest picture of life in Ireland.

Long may he continue to draw inspiration from the character and colour of this land which he loves so much. Our best wishes go with him and with Una, his wife. *Ian Kennedy.*

Grant Bremner

Grant Bremner joined the BBC in 1960, as an office junior in Aberdeen. After moving to London in 1963, he very quickly found a niche in the Music and Arts Gramophone Library, and just spent much of his career at the BBC there, moving from clerk to ATC, despite sorties to TFS as a trainee film assistant, to personnel, and to Lime Grove as an organiser in the early days of the Topical Production Centre. He took on the newly-created job of dresser manager in Costume Departments in 1984.

Grant will also be remembered for his work for the Association of Broadcasting Staff (ABS), later the Broadcasting Entertainments Trades Alliance (BETA). He first became a member of the Television Inter-branch Liaison Committee (later the Television Sub-divisional Committee) in 1970, was elected vice-chair in 1972 and chair from 1973 to 1980. He was a member of the National Executive Committee in various offices from 1974, to 1981. He was also chair of the Administration and Finance Committee from 1975 to 1981. Grant's detailed grasp of large and small matters and his formidable memory were remarkable.

Unfortunately, Grant has suffered from severe back problems for several years, and this has finally forced him from management team, and I am sure that all his friends and colleagues in the Television Service will want to join me in wishing him and his wife Sue, 'buen Suerte' and a happy future — perhaps in warmer climes. *J.S.*

Ian Keal

Ian Keal retires after 31 years service with the Corporation.

After studying Arabic at Durham University it was appropriate that Ian's permanent BBC job should be with the Arabic Service working both in production and administration. This period included a spell working in the Middle East Office.

Ian's forte proved to be in the areas of negotiation and diplomacy, evidenced by his achievements in Grading (later Pay Relativities) where he became head of department in 1978. His qualities of leadership, sound judgement and sensitivity to problems earned him the respect of BBC management and unions alike.

Ian's wealth of experience, charm and sense of humour will be missed by all his friends and colleagues who send their very best wishes for a full and happy retirement in Spain. *Roger Chase.*

Dave Fisher

Since coming to Pebble Mill in 1977 Dave Fisher has made many friends and been a valued and respected member of the security system.

Born in Durham, he has always managed to blend his Geordie wit with a conscientious approach to his duties. Using a firm but guiding hand Dave was able to stand literally above us all. He has a vast amount of experience to call upon with service in this country and as far afield as Africa.

Indeed the problems Dave has encountered while in the RAF with the African Man Mau must make parking and fire alarm problems at Pebble Mill seem rather insignificant but all were handled with the same true professionalism. He can now happily swop his uniform for a carpenter's apron and turn out the woodwork he so enjoys.

A devoted family man, our best wishes and thanks go to Dave and his wife Eunice. *R. Smith.*

Geoff McDonnell

Geoff McDonnell has retired early after 33 years in Transmission. He came to us after National Service in the RAF and three years in the telephone engineering branch of the General Post Office.

He spent the first 10 years travelling around transmitter sites as far apart as Wales and the Orkneys before settling at Kirk O'Shotts and latterly the new Black Hill base.

Geoff's wealth of experience and knowledge, particularly in locating sources of unobtainable spares, will be difficult to replace and his quiet humour will be greatly missed. We wish him a long and happy retirement. *Mike Barton.*

Paul Broad

Paul Broad joined the Skelton staff as a temporary storekeeper in 1981 and became a transport driver on the station in 1982. Following a reorganisation of the house services staff he was promoted to the post of supervisor in 1986.

Paul is sad to leave the service of the BBC. His colleagues will miss his particular style in dealing with their problems. He always tried to be fair and exercise mature judgement.

Our good wishes go to him and his wife, Jean, for a long, relaxed and happy retirement. *J.B. McKay.*

Norman Fawcett

With the early retirement of Norman Fawcett, over 50 years of a Transmitter Group presence on Anglesey came to an end with the closure of Llanddona as a manned base.

Norman joined the BBC after a number of years with Marconi and the New Zealand Shipping Company as a radio officer. He worked in Skelton, Redruth Oxford, Sandale and Fort William before joining the lotus eaters at Llanddona.

I am sure that his many friends in the BBC will wish him and his wife Betty a long and happy retirement. *Tys James.*

167

A Reference from Gary Richmond in case I required another job:

INDUSTRIAL RELATIONS SERVICE
PARAMOUNT HOUSE 162-170 WARDOUR STREET LONDON W1V 4LA TELEPHONE 01-494 4965 FAX: 01-734 4564

BRITISH FILM & TELEVISION PRODUCERS ASSOCIATION

BFTPA
IPPA

INDEPENDENT PROGRAMME PRODUCERS ASSOCIATION

W.G (Grant) Bremner

I am pleased to provide this reference for Mr W.G.(Grant) Bremner, for he is a person for whom I have the highest regard, both personally and professionally.

I have known Grant Bremner for nearly 20-years, our relationship being established within the BBC's Television Service. From the beginning I was impressed by his professional performance and by the manner in which he carried out his various roles. His capacity for understanding difficult issues, many of which had subtleties of a complex kind, was always apparent, as was his methodical, clear and calm approach towards everything he undertook. His very high professional reputation was fully justified and he met, unfailingly, the difficult and wide ranging demands of both senior management and production staff. He was frequently asked to contribute original ideas and his advice was taken more often than not.

Grant Bremner couples with the ability to work at high pressure, and at a senior level, an intellectual integrity of which he is entitled to be justly proud. In difficult situations he could be completely relied upon to act objectively and impartially, whilst, at the same time, bringing sound sense and understanding to the resolution of the problem. He also has a consuming belief in people and was known as a compassionate and articulate supporter of people who experienced difficulties.

In summary Grant Bremner is a man of sense and understanding who has a wealth of knowledge of handling important issues with both sensitivity and skill. His work for the BBC was of a very high standard and the Corporation has good reason to be grateful for much of what he did for them for nearly thirty years. He couples with his professional skills and experience personal attributes of a very high order.

I hold Grant Bremner in high regard and value his personal friendship as much as his professional role. I would unhesitatingly recommend him to you.

Gary Richmond
Director of Industrial Relations

That's nearly all folks.

Postscript:

I thought after my retirement party that I would have no more contact with the BBC other than visiting old friends. Sue and I went to live in Spain on the advice of my consultant after the third operation on my spine where he inserted Steffi Plates after removing two discs in an 8½ hour operation. He suggested that the warmth of the sun might help alleviate the pain, but more likely he probably just wanted to get rid of me. Unfortunately the sun did not work as I had a further three operations on my back in Spain.

However, in July of 1992 we were out shopping one day in Fuengirola when I spotted Andrew McKenzie, a Costume Designer I knew. After the pleasantries were over he then asked, 'Grant where can I buy a sewing machine?' Andrew was working on the ill-fated Eldorado programme that only lasted one year. We directed Andrew to an appropriate Spanish shop where he would find a number of sewing machines to choose from, and that was my last task for the BBC.

© 2023 Grant Bremner

Printed in Great Britain
by Amazon